TECHNICAL METHODS IN PHILOSOPHY

John L. Pollock

UNIVERSITY OF ARIZONA

Westview Press
BOULDER · SAN FRANCISCO · LONDON

Focus Series

Copyright © 1990 by Westview Press, Inc.

Published in 1990 in the United States of America by Westview Press, Inc., 5500 Central Avenue, Boulder, Colorado 80301, and in the United Kingdom by Westview Press, Inc., 13 Brunswick Centre, London WC1N 1AF, England

Library of Congress Cataloging-in-Publication Data
Pollock, John L.
    Technical methods in philosophy / by John L. Pollock.
        p. cm.—(The Focus series)
    ISBN 0-8133-7871-0. ISBN 0-8133-7872-9 (pbk.).
    1. Logic, Symbolic and mathematical. 2. Set theory. 3. Predicate
calculus. 4. First-order logic. 5. Metatheory. I. Title.
II. Series: Focus series (Westview Press)
BC135.P683 1990
160—dc20
                                                                89-38216
                                                                    CIP

Printed and bound in the United States of America

The paper used in this publication meets the requirements of the American
National Standard for Permanence of Paper for Printed Library Materials
Z39.48-1984.

10   9   8   7   6   5   4   3   2

For Carole

CONTENTS

PREFACE

The purpose of this book is to introduce the technical tools and concepts that are indispensable for advanced work in philosophy and to do so in a way that conveys the important concepts and techniques without becoming embroiled in unnecessary technical details. The most valuable technical tools are those provided by set theory and the predicate calculus. Knowledge of the predicate calculus is indispensable if for no other reason than that it is used so widely in the formulation of philosophical theories. This is partly because it has become conventional to formulate theories in that way, but it is also because the predicate calculus provides a medium for such formulations that is both concise and unambiguous. Furthermore, a knowledge of the predicate calculus is required for an understanding of Gödel's theorem. Gödel's theorem is one of the intellectually most important achievements of this century. Gödel's theorem and related theorems concerning the predicate calculus appear to have amazing implications for epistemology and the philosophy of mathematics. No student of philosophy can be regarded as properly educated without some grasp of these theorems.

An understanding of the predicate calculus requires some prior understanding of set theory. In addition, set theory is important in its own right. Set theory allows the concise and perspicuous formulation of principles that can only be formulated in a very complicated manner within nontechnical language. Given a basic grasp of set theoretic concepts, technical principles often become easy to understand, and it is easier to see what their logical consequences are. The same principles can be formulated in nontechnical language, but those formulations tend to become convoluted and unwieldy. A familiarity with set theoretic concepts also provides a different perspective from which to view abstract problems. The use of set theoretic concepts often reveals simple structure that would otherwise be concealed and helps one to think more clearly about the problems.

Nontechnical philosophers are often put off by the fact that set theory is generally developed as a foundation for mathematics. One begins with obscure axioms and derives formal theorems in a rigorous but unintuitive manner, with the ultimate objective of constructing theories of infinite cardinals and transfinite ordinals. For nontechnical philosophers, the theory of cardinals and ordinals is the least interesting part of set theory, and there is little point in developing set theory axiomatically. The axiomatic development of set theory is itself a response to a philosophical problem. That problem is fascinating, but it is most easily appreciated only after one has some grasp of set theory. Thus the current approach will be largely nonaxiomatic. More will be said about the philosophical significance of axiomatic set theory later in the book, but no attempt will be made here to discuss it in detail.

The emphasis in this book will be on those aspects of set theory and logic that are of most significance to the nonlogician. These include first the basic concepts of set theory like unions, intersections, relations, and functions. A sustained discussion of recursive definitions follows. This is a topic generally omitted from courses in set theory, and yet it is one of the most useful parts of set theory for the nonlogician. It is shown how the arithmetic of the natural numbers can be regarded as a simple consequence of the theory of recursive definitions. The chapter on the predicate calculus provides a concise presentation of model theory up through Gödel's theorem. Again, the emphasis is on conveying the philosophically important ideas rather than on working out all of the mathematical details. The book strives to be rigorous without going into unnecessary technical detail.

It is intended that one important audience for this book will consist of graduate students preparing for preliminary examinations in logic. Accordingly, I have tried to make the book intelligible to the reader who is working through it on his or her own without the help of an instructor. To that end, I have included exercises, and their solutions appear at the end of the book. In addition, there are a number of "practice exercises" whose only point is to give the reader additional practice with the concepts involved. Their solutions are left to the reader.

John L. Pollock
Telluride, Colorado

CHAPTER ONE
SET THEORY

1. The Logical Framework

Set theory is formulated using the notation of first order logic. It is assumed that the reader has a basic familiarity with the propositional and predicate calculi of the sort gained from a first course in symbolic logic. We use the following notation:

$(\forall x)$	universal quantifier
$(\exists x)$	existential quantifier
&	conjunction
$\vee$	disjunction
$\supset$	if ... then
$\equiv$	if and only if
$\sim$	negation
$=$	identity

It is assumed that the student has a working knowledge of which formulas of logic follow from which. That may not be a reasonable expectation in the case of identity, because identity is often omitted in beginning courses in logic. By 'identity' we mean 'numerical identity', not 'qualitative identity'. '$x = y$' means that x and y are literally the same thing. The basic principles regarding identity are simple and intuitive. All principles regarding identity in first order logic are consequences of the following four simple principles:

Reflexivity: $(\forall x)\ x = x$
        (Everything is identical to itself.)

Symmetry: $(\forall x)(\forall y)(x = y \supset y = x)$
>   (If one thing is identical to a second, then the second is identical to the first.)

Transitivity: $(\forall x)(\forall y)(\forall z)[(x = y \ \& \ y = z) \supset x = z]$
>   (If one thing is identical to a second, and the second is identical to a third, then the first is identical to the third.)

Substitutivity: $(\forall x)(\forall y)[x = y \supset (Ax \equiv Ay)]$
>   (If one thing is identical to a second, then anything true of the first is true of the second and vice versa.)

2. The Basic Concepts of Set Theory

A set, or class (these terms are used interchangeably here), is any collection of things. For example, one can talk about the set of all desks in the room, or the set of all past presidents, or the set of all non-negative integers.

2.1 Class Membership

The objects of which a set consists are its *members* or *elements*. We write 'x is a member of A' as '$x \in A$'. Similarly, we write 'x is not a member of A' as '$x \notin A$'. Note that we use upper case variables to range over sets, and lower case variables as general variables ranging over sets and non-sets alike. Thus '$(\forall X)FX$' means that all *sets* are F, whereas '$(\forall x)Fx$' means that *everything* is F. '$\in$' symbolizes the relation of *class membership*. All other relations between sets that are studied in set theory are defined in terms of this single basic relation.

Two sets are said to be the same set iff[1] they have the same members. This is expressed by the *axiom of extensionality*:

$$A = B \text{ iff } (\forall x)(x \in A \equiv x \in B)$$

---

[1] 'iff' is an abbreviation for 'if and only if'.

This provides a criterion of identity for sets. Notice in particular that the identity of a set is not determined by its defining property. The same set may have two or more quite different defining properties. For example, the set of all brick objects on campus may be the same set as the set of all buildings on campus, although these two defining properties are distinct.

2.2 Definition by Abstraction

By virtue of the axiom of extensionality, we can specify a set by saying what members it has. If a set is sufficiently small, we can do that by listing the members. We use the following notation:

Def: $\{a_1,...,a_n\}$ is the set whose members are just $a_1,...,a_n$.

If a set is large or infinite then we must specify its members in some other way, and that is typically done by giving a general description of its members. We use the following notation:

Def: $\{x \mid x$ is $F\}$ is the set whose members are all things having the property F.

This mode of specifying a set is called 'definition by abstraction'. As $\{x \mid x$ is $F\}$ is the set of all things having the property F, it follows that something has the property F iff it is a member of $\{x \mid x$ is $F\}$:

(2.1) $a \in \{x \mid x$ is $F\}$ iff a is F.

The question arises whether there is always such a set as $\{x \mid x$ is $F\}$. Intuitively, it seems that there should be. The principle affirming this is called *the axiom of comprehension*, and can be written as follows:

Given any property F, there is such a set as $\{x \mid x$ is $F\}$.

This axiom seems intuitively self-evident, and all of set theory can be developed on the basis of this axiom and the axiom of extensionality. It is rather astonishing, however, that despite its apparent self-evidence, the axiom of comprehension is logically inconsistent. This was first shown by Bertrand Russell, and the proof involves what has come to be known as 'Russell's paradox'. The proof is surprisingly simple, and goes as follows. We can construct sets whose members are other sets. For example, we might begin by constructing the two sets of numbers {1,2} and {2,3}, and then construct another set having just those sets as members: {{1,2},{2,3}}. Thus some sets can be members of other sets. The question arises whether any set can be a member of itself. If there is such a set as the set of all sets, then that set includes itself as a member, but clearly most sets will not be members of themselves. Consider the property of being a set that is not a member of itself. This is a property that most sets would seem to have. By the axiom of comprehension, there is a set of all sets having this property. Let us call it 'R':

$$R = \{X \mid X \notin X\}.$$

Now ask, is R a member of itself? By (2.1):

$$R \in R \text{ iff } R \notin R.$$

But by the propositional calculus, this is a contradiction. It implies that if R is a member of itself then it is not, and if it is not then it is. The only thing we have assumed in deriving this contradiction is that there is such a set R, and that is implied by the axiom of comprehension, so it follows that that seemingly self-evident axiom is actually inconsistent.

The inconsistency of the axiom of comprehension is perhaps the principal reason that set theory itself is philosophically interesting (as opposed to merely being philosophically useful). The axiom of comprehension seems so obvious that one is inclined to insist that it *must* be true, and yet Russell's demonstration is incontrovertible. The problem of the foundations of set theory is the problem of sorting this out. We would like to know why the axiom of comprehension is inconsistent when it seems self-evidently true, and we would like to know by what principles it should be replaced.

The general consensus is that the axiom of comprehension only fails in extraordinary instances. These instances comprise what are called *the set-theoretic antinomies*, and they are the subject of extensive investigation in the foundations of set theory. But for the purpose of developing set theory as a tool, we need not get involved in this. We can assume that the simple instances of the axiom of comprehension we are inclined to use are safe and unproblematic. For example, there is no problem constructing a set like the set of all buildings on campus. It is only when we consider very complicated sets of sets that danger looms. As long as we are reasonably conservative in our constructions, no problems will arise. Thus for most purposes, we can use definition by abstraction without much worry.

2.3 *Some Simple Sets*

It was noted that we can specify simple sets by listing their members, using the notation '$\{a_1,...,a_n\}$'. We could just as well have defined that notation using definition by abstraction:

$$\{a_1,...,a_n\} = \{x \mid x = a_1 \lor ... \lor x = a_n\}.$$

In the same way we can define the *unit set* of an object to be the set whose only member is that object:

Def: $\{a\} = \{x \mid x = a\}$.

A set that may seem initially puzzling is the *empty set*:

Def: $\emptyset = \{x \mid x \neq x\}$.

By (2.1), $x \in \emptyset$ iff $x \neq x$. But nothing has the property of not being self-identical, so it follows that nothing is a member of $\emptyset$ (hence its name). Initially, the empty set is apt to seem paradoxical. How can we have a collection without anything in it? But reflection shows that the empty set is not really so strange as it may first appear. For example, a mathematician might consider the set of all solutions to a particular equation, prove a number of theorems about that set, and ultimately establish that it is empty—the equation has no solutions. This would not move him to conclude that he has made a mistake in talking about the set of all solutions to the equation. The only reason the empty set sometimes seems strange is that in normal practice, if we know *antecedently* that there are no things satisfying a certain condition then we will not be inclined to form the set of all things satisfying that condition, but this is just because there would ordinarily be no point in doing so.

If we can define the empty set to be the set of everything that is not self-identical, then it might seem we should be able to define the *universal set* to be the set of everything that is self-identical:

$$U = \{x \mid x = x\}.$$

However, the universal set turns out to be implicated in the set-theoretic antinomies, so it is best not to assume that there is any such set.

2.4 Subsets

One of the most important relations between sets is that of *class inclusion*, or the *subset relation*. A set A is a subset ($\subseteq$) of B iff all of the members of A are also members of B:

Def: $A \subseteq B$ iff $(\forall x)(x \in A \supset x \in B)$.

The subset relation should not be confused with the membership relation. For example, suppose that a labor union can be identified with the set of its members. Let us further suppose that a local union is affiliated with a national union in such a way that all members of the local union are automatically members of the national union. Then the local union will be a subset of the national union. The local union will not be a member of the national union, but its members will be.

The following are a couple of obvious principles regarding subsets:

(2.2) $A \subseteq A$.   (reflexivity)

(2.3) $(A \subseteq B \ \& \ B \subseteq C) \supset A \subseteq C$.   (transitivity)

These principles follow directly from the definition of '$\subseteq$', using the predicate calculus. For instance, (2.3) is equivalent to saying that if all A's are B's and all B's are C's then all A's are C's. A principle that is only slightly less obvious is that if two sets are each subsets of each other, then they are identical:

(2.4) $(A \subseteq B \ \& \ B \subseteq A) \supset A = B.$

This is because if two sets are subsets of each other, then they have the same members, and so by the axiom of extensionality, they are the same set.

A principle that may at first seem surprising is that the empty set is a subset of every set:

(2.5) $\emptyset \subseteq A.$

This is because the empty set has no members, so it is automatically true that all members of the empty set are members of A. A frequent confusion here, related to the confusion of the membership relation with the subset relation, is to suppose that the empty set is a member of every set. For example, consider the set of all US senators. The empty set is not a senator, so the empty set is not a member of that set.

A helpful way of developing one's intuitions concerning relations between sets is with the use of Venn diagrams. We can represent a set diagrammatically as a circle, and represent the relations between sets in terms of topological relations between the circles. For example, we can diagram (2.3) by using concentric circles:

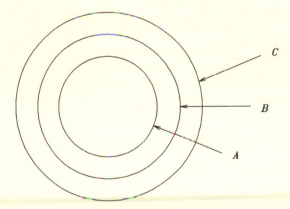

A is enclosed in B, indicating that $A \subseteq B$, and B is enclosed in C, indicating that $B \subseteq C$. Then it follows that A is also enclosed in C, and consequently $A \subseteq C$.

A slightly different relation between sets is that of *proper inclusion*. A is automatically a subset of B when A and B are the same set. In that case, B contains no members that are not also members of A. We say that A is a *proper subset* of B when $A \subseteq B$ but B contains at least one element that is not a member of A:

Def: $A \subset B$ iff $A \subseteq B$ & $(\exists x)(x \in B$ & $x \notin A)$.

Obviously, no set can be a proper subset of itself, because then it would have to contain an element that it does not contain:

(2.6) $\sim(A \subset A)$.

On the other hand, the proper subset relation is transitive:

(2.7) $(A \subset B$ & $B \subset C) \supset A \subset C$.

Proof: Suppose $A \subset B$ & $B \subset C$. Then $A \subseteq B$ & $B \subseteq C$, so by (2.3), $A \subseteq C$. What remains is to show that there is some element x of C that is not an element of A. As $B \subset C$, there is an element x of C that is not in B. Every element of A is an element of B, so x is not in A either.

Practice exercises:
1. $A \subset B$ iff $(A \subseteq B$ & $A \neq B)$.
2. If $A \subset B$ then $\sim(B \subset A)$.

2.5 Unions and Intersections
The *union* ($\cup$) of two sets consists of everything that is a member of at least one of the sets:

Def: $A \cup B = \{x \mid x \in A \vee x \in B\}$.

The union can be diagrammed as follows:

Similarly, the *intersection* (∩) of two sets consists of everything that is a member of both:

Def: $A∩B = \{x \mid x \in A \ \& \ x \in B\}$.

The intersection can be diagrammed as follows:

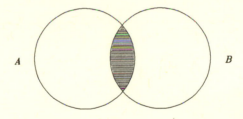

If $A∩B = \emptyset$, A and B are said to be *disjoint*. This means that they have no members in common.

A number of simple properties of unions and intersections are obvious. Any of these that do not seem obvious can be made obvious by drawing Venn diagrams:

(2.8) $A∩B = B∩A$; $A∪B = B∪A$.

(2.9) $(A∩B)∩C = A∩(B∩C)$; $(A∪B)∪C = A∪(B∪C)$.

(2.10) $A∪A = A∩A = A$.

(2.11) $A∩\emptyset = \emptyset$; $A∪\emptyset = A$.

(2.12) $A∩B \subseteq A$; $A \subseteq A∪B$.

The formal proofs of these principles in the predicate calculus are trivial, because each is equivalent to a simple theorem of the predicate calculus. For instance, the first half of (2.8) is equivalent to:

$$(\forall x)[(x \in A \ \& \ x \in B) \equiv (x \in B \ \& \ x \in A)].$$

Some simple principles are not immediately obvious but can be proven very simply:

(2.13) $A \subseteq B$ iff $A \cap B = A$.

Proof: If $A \subseteq B$ then those objects that are elements of both A and B are just those objects that are elements of A. Consequently, $A \cap B = A$. Conversely, suppose $A \cap B = A$. By (2.12), $A \cap B \subseteq B$, so if $A \cap B$ and A are the same set then $A \subseteq B$. (Note that what we are using here is the principle of the substitutivity of identity.)

The proofs of the following principles are similar:

(2.14) $A \subseteq B$ iff $A \cup B = B$.

Proof: exercise

(2.15) $A \subseteq B \ \& \ A \subseteq C$ iff $A \subseteq B \cap C$.

Proof: Suppose $A \subseteq B$ and $A \subseteq C$. To show that $A \subseteq B \cap C$ it suffices to show that $(\forall x)(x \in A \supset x \in B \cap C)$, so suppose $x \in A$. Then as $A \subseteq B$, $x \in B$, and as $A \subseteq C$, $x \in C$. Thus $x \in B \cap C$. This holds for arbitrary x, so $(\forall x)(x \in A \supset x \in B \cap C)$, i.e., $A \subseteq B \cap C$.
       Conversely, suppose $A \subseteq B \cap C$. By (2.12), $B \cap C \subseteq B$, so by transitivity (principle (2.3)), $A \subseteq B$. Similarly, $A \subseteq C$.

(2.16) $A \subseteq C \ \& \ B \subseteq C$ iff $A \cup B \subseteq C$.

Proof: exercise

The following two principles are most easily seen with the help of Venn diagrams:

(2.17) $(A \cup B) \cap C = (A \cap C) \cup (B \cap C)$.

(2.18) $(A \cap B) \cup C = (A \cup C) \cap (B \cup C)$.

2.6 Relative Complements

The *complement of B relative to A* is the set of all members of A that are not members of B:

Def: $A - B = \{x \mid x \in A \,\&\, x \notin B\}$.

$A - B$ can be diagrammed as follows:

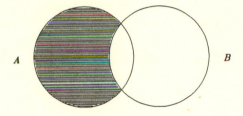

The following two theorems are called *De Morgan's Laws*:

(2.19) $A - (B \cup C) = (A - B) \cap (A - C)$.

Proof: This follows from De Morgan's laws in the propositional calculus:

$$x \in A - (B \cup C) \text{ iff } x \in A \,\&\, x \notin B \cup C)$$
$$\text{iff } x \in A \,\&\, \sim(x \in B \lor x \in C)$$
$$\text{iff } x \in A \,\&\, x \notin B \,\&\, x \notin C$$
$$\text{iff } (x \in A \,\&\, x \notin B) \,\&\, (x \in A \,\&\, x \notin C)$$
$$\text{iff } x \in (A - B) \,\&\, x \in (A - C)$$
$$\text{iff } x \in (A - B) \cap (A - C)$$

(2.20) $A - (B \cap C) = (A - B) \cup (A - C)$.

Proof: exercise

Practice exercise: $A - (A \cap B) = A - B$.

2.7 *Power Sets*

Union, intersection, and complement are *set-theoretic opera-tions*. Set-theoretic operations generate new sets from old. The operations we have considered so far generate sets of the "same level" as those with which we begin. For instance, if A and B are sets of physical objects, so are $A \cap B$, $A \cup B$, and $A - B$. The next operation "moves us up a level", in the sense that if we begin with a set of physical objects, what we end up with is a set of sets of physical objects. This operation is the *power set* operation. The power set (**P**) of a set is the collection of all of its subsets:

Def: $\mathbf{P}(A) = \{X \mid X \subseteq A\}$.

The reason for the name is that if A contains n members, then $\mathbf{P}(A)$ contains 2^n members.

By virtue of the definition:

(2.21) $X \in \mathbf{P}(A)$ iff $X \subseteq A$.

Consequently:

(2.22) $A \in \mathbf{P}(A)$.

(2.23) $\emptyset \in \mathbf{P}(A)$.

(2.24) $\mathbf{P}(\emptyset) = \{\emptyset\}$.

Proof: $\emptyset$ is the only subset of $\emptyset$, so it is the only member of $\mathbf{P}(\emptyset)$.

(2.25) $A \subseteq B$ iff $\mathbf{P}(A) \subseteq \mathbf{P}(B)$.

Proof: Suppose $A \subseteq B$. Then by transitivity, every subset of A is a subset of B, and hence $\mathbf{P}(A) \subseteq \mathbf{P}(B)$. Conversely, suppose $\mathbf{P}(A) \subseteq \mathbf{P}(B)$. Then every subset of A is a subset of B. But $A \subseteq A$, so $A \subseteq B$.

(2.26) $\mathbf{P}(A \cap B) = \mathbf{P}(A) \cap \mathbf{P}(B)$.

Proof: exercise   (Hint: use (2.15))

Exercise: It is not always true that $\mathbf{P}(A) \cup \mathbf{P}(B) = \mathbf{P}(A \cup B)$. What are simple necessary and sufficient conditions for this identity to hold?

2.8 Generalized Union and Intersection

Given a class K of sets, the generalized intersection ($\bigcap$) of K consists of those elements that all members of K have in common, and the generalized union ($\bigcup$) of K consists of all elements that occur in at least one member of K:

Def: $\bigcap K = \{x \mid (\forall Y)(Y \in K \supset x \in Y)\}$.

Def: $\bigcup K = \{x \mid (\exists Y)(Y \in K \,\&\, x \in Y)\}$.

$\bigcap K$ is the set that results from intersecting all of the sets in K, and $\bigcup K$ is the set that results from forming the union of all the sets in K. For instance, if $K = \{\{1,2,3\},\{2,3,4\},\{3,4,5\}\}$, then $\bigcap K = \{3\}$ and $\bigcup K = \{1,2,3,4,5\}$. In general:

(2.27) If $K = \{A_1,...,A_n\}$ then $\bigcap K = A_1 \cap ... \cap A_n$ and $\bigcup K = A_1 \cup ... \cup A_n$.

Here are some simple theorems regarding generalized union and intersection:

(2.28) $\bigcup \emptyset = \emptyset$.

Proof: The members of $\bigcup \emptyset$ are those things that are members of at least one member of $\emptyset$. But $\emptyset$ has no members, so $\bigcup \emptyset$ has no members.

(2.29) $\bigcup \{A\} = A$.

Proof: exercise

(2.30) $\bigcup (H \cup K) = (\bigcup H) \cup (\bigcup K)$.

Proof: $x \in \bigcup (H \cup K)$ iff $(\exists Y)[x \in Y \,\&\, Y \in H \cup K]$
  iff $(\exists Y)[x \in Y \,\&\, (Y \in H \,\vee\, Y \in K)]$
  iff $(\exists Y)[(x \in Y \,\&\, Y \in H) \,\vee\, (x \in Y \,\&\, Y \in K)]$

iff $(\exists Y)(x \in Y \;\&\; Y \in H) \lor (\exists Y)(x \in Y \;\&\; Y \in K)$
iff $x \in \bigcup H \lor x \in UK$
iff $x \in (\bigcup H) \cup (\bigcup K)$.

(2.31)   If $H \subseteq K$ then $\bigcup H \subseteq \bigcup K$.

Proof: exercise

(2.32)   If $(\forall X)(X \in K \supset X \subseteq A)$ then $\bigcup K \subseteq A$.

Proof: Suppose $(\forall X)(X \in K \supset X \subseteq A)$. Suppose $x \in \bigcup K$. Then for some X in K, $x \in X$. But if $X \in K$, $X \subseteq A$, so $x \in A$. Hence $\bigcup K \subseteq A$.

Theorem (2.32) can be diagrammed as follows:

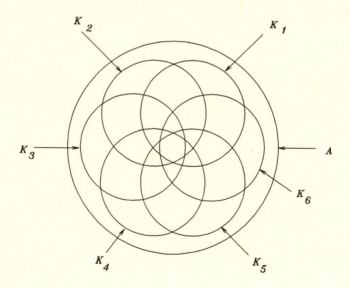

(2.33) $\bigcap \{A\} = A$.

Proof: exercise

(2.34)   If $H \subseteq K$ then $\bigcap K \subseteq \bigcap H$.

Proof: exercise

(2.35)   If $A \in K$ then $\bigcap K \subseteq A$.

Proof: exercise

(2.36)   If $(\forall X)(X \in K \supset A \subseteq X)$ then $A \subseteq \bigcap K$.

Proof: exercise

Practice exercises:
1. $\bigcup(H \cap K) \subseteq (\bigcup H) \cap (\bigcup K)$.
2. $\bigcap(H \cup K) = (\bigcap H) \cap (\bigcap K)$.
3. $\bigcup \mathbf{P}(A) = A$.
4. $\bigcup K \subseteq B$ iff $K \subseteq \mathbf{P}(B)$.

3.   Relations

What contributes to the usefulness of set theory more than anything else is its ability to handle relations and functions. The key to this is the concept of an ordered pair.

3.1 Ordered Pairs

Perhaps the original motivation for the concept of an ordered pair comes from mathematics, where we want to talk about a point in a plane being determined by its coordinates. Each point in the plane is associated with a pair of values, the first of which is the point's position relative to the x-axis and the second of which is its position relative to the y-axis. In specifying the coordinates it makes a difference which value comes first. The point associated with the coordinates 3,4 is different from the point associated with 4,3. Here we are dealing with ordered pairs of coordinate values, because the order in which the values are listed makes a difference. The ordered pair 3,4 cannot be identified with the set {3,4}, because the order in which the elements of the latter set are listed makes no difference to the identity of the set: {3,4} = {4,3}.

Pointed brackets '⟨' and '⟩' are used when referring to ordered pairs. For example, ⟨3,4⟩ is the ordered pair whose first member is 3 and whose second member is 4. An ordered pair $\langle a,b \rangle$ is a new sort of entity distinct from the unordered pair $\{a,b\}$. The identity of an unordered pair is determined by its members. The identity of an ordered pair, on the other hand, is determined by two things—its members and their order. This is captured by the following principle:

(3.1) $\langle x,y \rangle = \langle z,w \rangle$ iff $x = z$ & $y = w$.

In order to incorporate ordered pairs into set theory, we could simply adopt the concept of an ordered pair as a new undefined concept and take (3.1) as an axiom analogous to the axiom of extensionality for unordered sets. That is not the way it is generally done, however. Instead of taking ordered pairs as primitive, it is possible to construct sets that "work like ordered pairs", in the sense of satisfying (3.1), and ordered pairs are then identified with these constructed sets. The thing to be emphasized here is that the only principle regarding ordered pairs about which we care is that they satisfy (3.1), so any definition that results in their satisfying (3.1) is as good as any other. Several different constructions are known. The most popular is due to Kuratowski. First, we prove:

(3.2) $\{\{x\},\{x,y\}\} = \{\{z\},\{z,w\}\}$ iff $x = z$ & $y = w$.

Proof: By the substitutivity of identity, if $x = z$ & $y = w$ then $\{\{x\},\{x,y\}\} = \{\{z\},\{z,w\}\}$. Conversely, suppose $\{\{x\},\{x,y\}\} = \{\{z\},\{z,w\}\}$. Then these sets have the same elements, so one of two things must be the case. Either (1) $\{x\} = \{z\}$ and $\{x,y\} = \{z,w\}$, or (2) $\{x\} = \{z,w\}$ and $\{x,y\} = \{z\}$. Suppose (1) is the case. As $\{x\} = \{z\}$, these sets must have the same members, so $x = z$. Then $\{x,y\} = \{z,y\}$. Furthermore, as $\{x,y\} = \{z,w\}$, we can conclude that $\{z,y\} = \{z,w\}$. Then either (i) $y = w$, or (ii) $z = w$ and $y = z$. But in either case, $y = w$. Thus if (1) holds, $x = z$ and $y = w$. On the other hand, suppose (2) holds. As $\{x\} = \{z,w\}$, then $x = z = w$. And as $\{x,y\} = \{z\}$ we have $x = y = z$. Thus $x = y = z = w$. Consequently $x = z$ and $y = w$. Thus regardless of whether (1) is the case or (2) is the case, $x = z$ and $y = w$.

By virtue of theorem (3.2), $\{\{x\},\{x,y\}\}$ works the way we want the ordered pair $\langle x,y\rangle$ to work. For this reason, ordered pairs are generally identified with such unordered sets, absolving us from taking ordered pairs as a new primitive concept:

Def: $\langle x,y\rangle = \{\{x\},\{x,y\}\}$.

It should be understood that this is really no more than a technical trick. There is no sense in which ordered pairs are "really" such unordered sets. Rather, we have found something that works like an ordered pair, so we use that. We could just as well have used, for example, $\{\{\{x\}\},\{\{x\},\{y\}\}\}$.

The *Cartesian product* ($\times$) of two sets A and B is the set of all ordered pairs where the first member is taken from A and the second member is taken from B:

Def: $A{\times}B = \{\langle x,y\rangle \mid x{\in}A \ \& \ y{\in}B\}$.

For example, if $A = \{1,2\}$ and $B = \{3,4\}$ then $A{\times}B = \{\langle 1,3\rangle,\langle 1,4\rangle,\langle 2,3\rangle,\langle 2,4\rangle\}$. The Cartesian product of two sets can be diagrammed as follows:

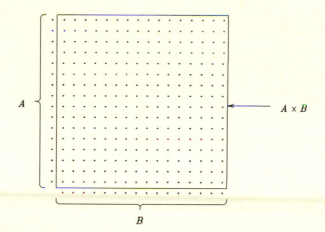

This sort of diagram makes it easy to see that the following theorem is true:

(3.3) $A \times B = \emptyset$ iff either $A = \emptyset$ or $B = \emptyset$.

(3.4)   If $A \neq \emptyset$ & $B \neq \emptyset$ then $A \times B = C \times D$ iff $A = C$ & $B = D$.

Proof: exercise

(3.5) $A \times (B \cup C) = (A \times B) \cup (A \times C)$.

Proof: exercise

Practice exercises:
1. $A \times (B \cap C) = (A \times B) \cap (A \times C)$.
2. $(A \times B) \cap (C \times D) = (A \cap C) \times (B \cap D)$.
3. $(A \times B) \cup (C \times D) \subseteq (A \cup C) \times (B \cup D)$.

3.2 Ordered n-tuples

In addition to the concept of an ordered pair, it is convenient to have the concept of an ordered triple, an ordered quadruple, etc. In general, an ordered set of length n is called *an ordered n-tuple*. There are different ways of defining ordered n-tuples, but one way of doing it is to take an ordered triple to be an ordered pair whose first member is an ordered pair, an ordered quadruple to be an ordered pair whose first member is an ordered triple, and so on:

Def: $\langle a_1, a_2, a_3 \rangle = \langle \langle a_1, a_2 \rangle, a_3 \rangle$
          $\langle a_1, a_2, a_3, a_4 \rangle = \langle \langle a_1, a_2, a_3 \rangle, a_4 \rangle$
          .
          .
          .
          $\langle a_1, ..., a_{n+1} \rangle = \langle \langle a_1, a_2, ... \rangle, a_{n+1} \rangle$

This has the result that for any $n \geq 2$, an ordered n-tuple is also an ordered pair. In general, if $m < n$ then an ordered n-tuple is also an ordered m-tuple.

We will frequently want to talk about ordered n-tuples for unspecified n, *including* the case in which $n = 1$. Strictly as a technical convenience, we will identify the ordered one-tuple $\langle x \rangle$ with x itself.

3.3 *The Extensions of Properties and Relations*

Properties are "intensional items" in the sense that two distinct properties can be possessed by precisely the same objects. This can be expressed by saying that two distinct properties can have the same extensions. The *extension* of a property is the set of all objects possessing that property:

Def: If F is a property, the extension of F is $\{x \mid x$ is $F\}$.

For instance, the property of being a unicorn is a different property than that of being a winged horse, but presumably the extension of each is the empty set.

As the term 'relation' is used outside of set theory, relations are analogous to properties in that they too are intensional items. Two distinct relations could be such that the same objects stand in those relations to one another. This can be expressed by saying that two distinct relations can have the same extension. But the notion of the extension of a relation must be more complicated than the notion of the extension of a property. The extension of a two-place relation cannot be a set of individuals, because a relation does not deal with single individuals. Rather, a two-place relation deals with ordered pairs of individuals. For example, if we write, "John is taller than Bill" we are saying that the first member of the ordered pair ⟨John,Bill⟩ stands in the relation 'is taller than' to the second member. This suggests that we think of a two-place relation as a property of ordered pairs. For example, we can think of the relation 'is taller than' as a property possessed by all ordered pairs ⟨x,y⟩ such that x is taller than y. Thinking of relations in this way leads to the standard definition of the extension of a relation:

Def: If R is a two-place relation, the extension of R is $\{⟨x,y⟩ \mid$ x stands in the relation R to $y\}$.

Not all relations are two-place relations. For example, 'is between' is a three-place relation. In general, the extension of an n-place relation can be regarded as a set of ordered n-tuples:

Def: If R is an n-place relation, the extension of R is $\{⟨x_1,...,x_n⟩ \mid x_1,...,x_n$ stand in the relation R to one another$\}$.

A special case of this definition occurs when $n = 1$. One-place relations are properties, and the extension of a one-place relation P is then the set of all one-tuples $\langle x \rangle$ such that x has the property P. But we have identified $\langle x \rangle$ with x, so this coincides with our initial definition of the extension of a property.

It turns out that for most purposes, anything we want to say about a relation can be reformulated as a statement about its extension. For example, rather than say that John stands in the relation 'is taller than' to Bill, we can say that $\langle$John,Bill$\rangle$ is a member of the extension of the relation 'is taller than'. It is this that makes set theory such a handy vehicle for talk about relations. For the purposes of set theory, *relations are identified with their extensions*. A two-place relation becomes a set of ordered pairs, a three-place relation becomes a set of ordered triples, and so on.

This section began with the observation that relations are intensional items that can be distinct while having the same extension, but we have now adopted a definition that has the opposite consequence. If relations *are* their extensions, then obviously distinct relations cannot have the same extension. This is a bit confusing. To resolve the confusion it is customary to distinguish between *relations in intension* and *relations in extension*. Relations in intension are the sorts of things that are analogous to properties of ordered pairs. Relations in extension are sets of ordered pairs. Thus the extension of a relation in intension is a relation in extension. In set theory, when we say 'relation' without qualification, we mean 'relation in extension'. Precisely:

Def: R is a relation iff R is a set of ordered pairs.

Still, there is the danger of philosophical confusion here. Identifying relations with their extensions is not sufficient to justify this definition. That identification makes a relation a set of ordered pairs, but does it make every set of ordered pairs a relation? This turns upon the question whether every set of ordered pairs is the extension of a relation in intension. It is not obvious that this is so. For example, we might have some strange infinite set of ordered pairs of numbers. Will there always be a relation having such an extension? Part of the difficulty in answering this question concerns the notion of a relation in intension. It is not clear what the limits are on what relations in

intension there are. For example, must relations in intension be
in principle "mentally graspable"? Set theory tries to avoid this
question rather than answering it, and it does this by simply
stipulating that, for purposes of set theory, what is meant by
'relation' is 'set of ordered pairs'. It is not clear, however, that this
is entirely legitimate. The problem is that in some cases we want
to establish the existence of a relation with certain properties (this
is particularly true in mathematics). But without an affirmative
answer to the question, "Is every set of ordered pairs the extension
of a relation in intension?", establishing the existence of a relation
in extension does not automatically establish the existence of a
relation in intension having that extension. Thus it is not always
clear that existence theorems in set theory have the significance
they seem to have.

   Having expressed the above reservations, I will proceed to use
the term 'relation' as is customary in set theory. We can define
more generally:

Def: R is an n-place relation iff R is a set of ordered n-tuples.

Because ordered n-tuples are also ordered pairs, every relation is
a two-place relation. Similarly, if $m < n$ then every n-place
relation is also an m-place relation.

   To make our notation more perspicuous, it is convenient to
define:

Def: xRy iff $\langle x,y \rangle \in R$.

3.4 Operations on Relations

   The *domain* of a relation is the set of all things that stand in
that relation to something:

Def: $\mathbf{D}(R) = \{x \mid (\exists y)xRy\}$.

Analogously, the *range* of a relation is the set of all things to which
the relation relates something:

Def: $\mathbf{R}(R) = \{y \mid (\exists x)xRy\}$.

The *field* of a relation is the union of the domain and range:

Def: $F(R) = D(R) \cup R(R)$.

To illustrate, consider the 'less than' relation on the positive integers (the integers greater than zero). The domain of this relation is the set of all positive integers. As there are no positive integers less than one, the range of this relation is the set of all integers greater than one. And the field is the set of all positive integers.

If R is a relation, the R-image of a set A is the set of all things related to members of A by R:

Def: $R^*A = \{y \mid (\exists x)(x \in A \ \& \ xRy\}$.

The range of R is just the R-image of the domain of R:

(3.6) $R^*D(R) = R(R)$.

A couple of elementary theorems follow:

(3.7) $R^*(A \cup B) = (R^*A) \cup (R^*B)$.

Proof: exercise

(3.8)   If $A \subseteq B$ then $R^*A \subseteq R^*B$.

Proof: exercise

The *converse* of a relation is the relation that results from turning the first relation around:

Def: $R^{-1} = \{\langle x,y \rangle \mid yRx\}$.

For example, the converse of 'is taller than' is 'is shorter than'. The converse of the converse of a relation is the original relation:

(3.9)   If R is a relation then $(R^{-1})^{-1} = R$.

Proof: $(R^{-1})^{-1} = \{\langle x,y \rangle \mid \langle y,x \rangle \in R^{-1}\} = \{\langle x,y \rangle \mid \langle x,y \rangle \in R\} = R$.

Cartesian products are relations, and the converse of a Cartesian product is obtained by taking the product in the reverse order:

(3.10) $(A \times B)^{-1} = B \times A$.

Proof: exercise

Taking the converse of a relation reverses the domain and range:

(3.11) $\mathbf{D}(R^{-1}) = \mathbf{R}(R)$ & $\mathbf{R}(R^{-1}) = \mathbf{D}(R)$.

The *relative product* of two relations is defined as follows:

Def: $R/S = \{\langle x,z \rangle \mid (\exists y)(xRy \text{ \& } ySz)\}$.

Schematically, $x(R/S)y$ means that for some y, $xRySz$. For example, if R is the relation 'is the mother of' and S is the relation 'is a parent of' then R/S is 'is the mother of some parent of', i.e., 'is a grandmother of'.

Practice exercises:
1. $\mathbf{D}(R \cup S) = \mathbf{D}(R) \cup \mathbf{D}(S)$.
2. $\mathbf{R}(R \cup S) = \mathbf{R}(R) \cup \mathbf{R}(S)$.
3. $R^*(A \cap B) \subseteq R^*(A) \cap R^*(B)$.
4. $(R/S)/T = R/(S/T)$.
5. $(R/S)^{-1} = (S^{-1})/(R^{-1})$.
6. $R/(S \cup T) = (R/S) \cup (R/T)$.

3.5   *Properties of Relations*
There are a number of important properties that relations may have. Let us define:

Def: R is reflexive iff $(\forall x)[x \in \mathbf{F}(R) \supset xRx]$.

Def: R is irreflexive iff $(\forall x) \sim xRx$.

Def: R is symmetric iff $(\forall x)(\forall y)(xRy \supset yRx)$.

Def: R is asymmetric iff $(\forall x)(\forall y)(xRy \supset \sim yRx)$.

Def: R is antisymmetric iff $(\forall x)(\forall y)[(xRy \mathbin{\&} x \neq y) \supset {\sim}yRx]$.

Def: R is transitive iff $(\forall x)(\forall y)(\forall z)[(xRy \mathbin{\&} yRz) \supset xRz]$.

Def: R is connected iff $(\forall x)(\forall y)[x,y{\in}F(R) \supset (xRy \lor yRx \lor x = y)]$.[2]

Def: R is strongly connected iff $(\forall x)(\forall y)[x,y{\in}F(R) \supset (xRy \lor yRx)]$.

To illustrate, let '<' be the 'less than' relation on the integers, and let '≤' be the 'less than or equal to' relation on the integers. < is irreflexive, asymmetrical, transitive, and connected. ≤ on the other hand is reflexive, antisymmetric, transitive, and strongly connected.
    There are a number of connections between these properties. For instance:

(3.12)   If R is transitive and symmetric then R is reflexive.

Proof: Suppose R is transitive and symmetric. Suppose $x{\in}F(R)$. Then either $x{\in}D(R)$ or $x{\in}R(R)$. If $x{\in}D(R)$ then there is a y such that xRy. Then by symmetry, yRx. Then by transitivity, as xRy and yRx, it follows that xRx. Analogously, if $x{\in}R(R)$ then xRx. Consequently, R is reflexive.

(3.13)   If R is asymmetric then R is irreflexive.

Proof: exercise

Practice exercise: Show that if R is, respectively, reflexive, irreflexive, symmetric, asymmetric, antisymmetric, transitive, connected, or strongly connected, then R^{-1} is, respectively, reflexive, irreflexive, symmetric, asymmetric, antisymmetric, transitive, connected, or strongly connected.

---

[2] We write '$x,y{\in}F(R)$' as an abbreviation for '$x{\in}F(R) \mathbin{\&} y{\in}F(R)$'.

3.6 Equivalence Relations

If there were such a thing as the 'identity relation', it would be $\{\langle x,y \rangle \mid x = y\}$. For reasons pertaining to the set-theoretic antinomies, it is generally granted that there is no such set, and hence no such relation (in extension). However, given any set A we can construct a relation that we can call 'the identity relation on A':

Def: $Id_A = \{\langle x,y \rangle \mid x,y \in A \ \& \ x = y\}$.

Id_A can be completely characterized by saying that it is transitive, symmetric, and satisfies the substitutivity condition:

$$\langle x,y \rangle \in Id_A \supset (\forall X)(x \in X \equiv y \in X).$$

Equivalence relations are those relations that have all of the algebraic properties of Id_A but do not necessarily satisfy the substitutivity condition:

Def: R is an equivalence relation iff R is a relation and R is transitive and symmetric.

For instance, the relation 'is the same height as' is an equivalence relation. In light of (3.12):

(3.14)   If R is an equivalence relation then R is reflexive.

An equivalence relation divides its field into disjoint subsets called 'equivalence classes', such that within each equivalence class all the elements are equivalent, and no elements in different equivalence classes are equivalent. The *R-equivalence class of x* is the set of all things equivalent under R to x. This is simply the *R*-image of x, $R^*\{x\}$. Common notations for the R-equivalence class of x are '$R[x]$' and '$[x]_R$'. The following theorem tells us that all elements of a given equivalence class are equivalent, and no elements of different equivalence classes are equivalent:

(3.15)   If R is an equivalence relation and $x,y \in F(R)$ then $R^*\{x\} = R^*\{y\}$ iff xRy.

Proof: Suppose R is an equivalence relation and $x,y \in F(R)$. By (3.14), R is reflexive, so yRy. Thus $y \in R^*\{y\}$. Then if $R^*\{x\} = R^*\{y\}$, it follows that $y \in R^*\{x\}$, and hence xRy. Conversely, suppose xRy. Suppose $z \in R^*\{x\}$. Then xRz. As xRy, we have by symmetry that yRx, and then by transitivity that yRz. Thus $z \in R^*\{y\}$. Therefore, $R^*\{x\} \subseteq R^*\{y\}$. Analogously, $R^*\{y\} \subseteq R^*\{x\}$, so $R^*\{x\} = R^*\{y\}$.

Different equivalence classes are disjoint:

(3.16) If R is an equivalence relation and $x,y \in F(R)$ and $R^*\{x\} \neq R^*\{y\}$ then $R^*\{x\} \cap R^*\{y\} = \emptyset$.

Proof: exercise

   A *partition* of a set is a collection of disjoint non-empty subsets of a set that collectively exhaust all of the members of the set:

Def: K is a partition of A iff
         (1) $(\forall X)(X \in K \supset X \neq \emptyset)$;
         (2) $(\forall X)(\forall Y)[(X,Y \in K \ \& \ X \neq Y) \supset X \cap Y = \emptyset]$; and
         (3) $\bigcup K = A$.

We can think of a partition of A as dividing A into disjoint cells:

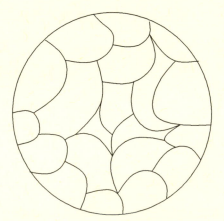

If R is an equivalence relation then the set of R-equivalence classes constitutes a partition of $\mathbf{F}(R)$. Conversely, each partition of a set generates an equivalence relation, namely, the relation between two objects of being in the same element of the partition.

Practice exercises:
1. If R is an equivalence relation, then $\{R^*\{x\} \mid x \in \mathbf{F}(R)\}$ is a partition of $\mathbf{F}(R)$.
2. If K is a partition of A then $\{\langle x,y \rangle \mid (\exists X)(X \in K \;\&\; x,y \in X)\}$ is an equivalence relation.

3.7 Ordering Relations

The set of natural numbers (that is, the positive integers together with zero) is called 'ω'. The set ω is said to be *linearly ordered* by the '$\leq$' relation. This means that the members of ω can be arranged in a single line and then for any integers n and m, it can be read off from the positions of n and m on the line whether $m \leq n$:

$$0 \; 1 \; 2 \; 3 \; 4 \; 5 \; ... \; n \; ... \; m \; ...$$

The official name for such a linear ordering is 'simple ordering'. Simple orderings are characterized by four properties:

Def: R is a simple ordering iff R is a relation and R is transitive, reflexive, antisymmetric, and strongly connected.

That simple orderings always arrange the elements of their field linearly can be seen as follows. Suppose R is transitive. This means that if we draw arrows between the elements of the field of R when they stand in the relation R to one another, we get lines (with the direction indicated by the arrows) such that anything to the left of something else on a given line stands in the relation R to it:

Suppose R is also antisymmetric. Then if x is to the left of y on a line, y is not also to the left of x, i.e., the line does not go around in a circle. If in addition R is strongly connected, then everything in its field lies on a single line. Finally, if R is reflexive then everything is related to itself, so R is analogous to '≤' rather than '<'.

If we look at the relation '<' on ω, it is not a simple ordering. It is instead what will be called a *strict simple ordering*:

Def: R is a strict simple ordering iff R is a relation and R is transitive, asymmetric, and connected.

By theorem (3.13), a strict simple ordering is automatically irreflexive. The difference between a simple ordering and a strict simple ordering is that the simple ordering relates everything to itself (it is reflexive) and the strict simple ordering is irreflexive. This is captured by the following two theorems:

(3.17)   If R is a strict simple ordering then $R \cup \{\langle x,x \rangle \mid x \in F(R)\}$ is a simple ordering.

(3.18)   If R is a simple ordering then $R - \{\langle x,x \rangle \mid x \in F(R)\}$ is a strict simple ordering.

Theorem (3.17) says that if we add to R all ordered pairs $\langle x,x \rangle$ for x in $F(R)$, thus constructing a relation identical to R except that it is also reflexive, we obtain a simple ordering. And theorem (3.18) tells us that if we start with a simple ordering and remove all those pairs $\langle x,x \rangle$, what is left is a strict simple ordering. The proofs of these theorems are left as an exercise.

Both simple orderings and strict simple orderings arrange the elements of their field linearly, and are called 'linear orderings'. Unfortunately, terminology is not uniform throughout set theory and in many texts strict simple orderings are called 'simple orderings'.

A weaker kind of ordering is a *partial ordering*. Instead of arranging the elements of its field on a single line, a partial ordering arranges them on several possibly branching lines. For example, a partial ordering might look like this:

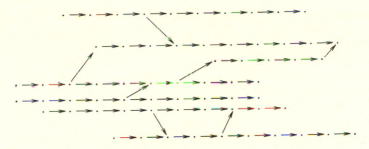

The difference between a simple ordering and a partial ordering is that a partial ordering is not strongly connected:

Def: R is a partial ordering iff R is a relation and R is transitive, reflexive, and antisymmetric.

For example, consider the subset relation between subsets of some given set A:

$$\subseteq_A = \{\langle X,Y \rangle \mid X \subseteq A \ \& \ Y \subseteq A \ \& \ X \subseteq Y\}.$$

This relation is a partial ordering. It is obviously transitive, reflexive, and antisymmetric, but it is not strongly connected because it is not automatically true that given any two subsets of A, one will be a subset of the other.

A strict partial ordering is like a partial ordering except that it is irreflexive instead of reflexive:

Def: R is a strict partial ordering iff R is a relation and R is transitive and asymmetric.

(Recall that by (3.13), asymmetry guarantees irreflexivity.) An example of a strict partial ordering is the proper subset relation between subsets of some given set A:

$$\subset_A = \{\langle X,Y \rangle \mid X \subseteq A \ \& \ Y \subseteq A \ \& \ X \subset Y\}.$$

Another example is the relation 'is an ancestor of'.

The final kind of ordering relation that we will consider is a *well ordering*. A well ordering is a special kind of simple ordering.

It is best explained by contrasting the ordering of ω by $\leq$ and the ordering of the set of all real numbers Rl by $\leq$. Given any nonempty set of integers, there is always a first member of that set. But this is not true of sets of real numbers. There can be nonempty sets of real numbers that do not have first members. For example, consider the set of all real numbers larger than 1 but less than 2. There is no smallest real number larger than 1, so this set has no first member. A well ordering is a simple ordering in which every nonempty set of elements has a first member. So the integers are well ordered by $\leq$ but the real numbers are not. To make this precise, we define:

Def: x is an R-first element of A iff $x \in A$ and $(\forall y)(y \in A \supset xRy)$.

Def: x is a well ordering iff R is a simple ordering and every nonempty subset of $\mathbf{F}(R)$ has an R-first element.

Well orderings are of importance because if a set is well ordered we can think of its members being linearly ordered in such a way that each element has a place marked by an ordinal number. In that case we can talk about the first member, the second member, etc. It is a generalization of this that leads to the notion of a transfinite ordinal number. Transfinite ordinals mark places in infinite well ordered sets. This is a matter of great interest in set theory, but we will not pursue it in detail here.

4. Functions

A function is a mapping of objects onto objects. To each object in its domain a function assigns a unique value (another object). For example, to each natural number the function $(x+1)$ assigns the next larger number. Similarly, to each person the function 'the father of x' assigns a particular person—his father. Corresponding to each one-place function f is a two-place relation R_f such that 'x stands in the relation R_f to y' is equivalent to '$f(x) = y$'. A relation R_f obtained in this way from a function will have the characteristic that for each object x in its domain, there is only one thing y to which x stands in the relation R_f; y must be $f(x)$. Such relations are called *functional relations*. Corresponding to each function is a functional relation. Next, notice that corresponding to each functional relation R (relation in intension, not extension) is a function f_R where '$f_R(x) = y$' is equivalent to 'y is the unique thing that stands in the relation R to x'. Furthermore, for any function f,

$$f_{(R_f)} = f,$$

i.e., the function that corresponds to the functional relation that is obtained from the original function is the original function itself. This correspondence between functions and functional relations justifies our identifying a function with its corresponding relation. Thus the terms 'function' and 'functional relation' will be used interchangeably.

Notice that our reservations about whether every relation in extension is the extension of a relation in intension carry over to functions. Let us define a *function in extension* to be a relation in extension that satisfies the condition that each object in its domain is related to exactly one object in its range:

Def: R is a function in extension iff R is a relation in extension and $(\forall x)[x \in D(R) \supset$ there is a unique y such that $xRy]$.

Clearly, the extension of a function (a functional relation in intension) is always a function in extension, but for the reasons discussed earlier it is not clear whether every function in extension is the extension of a function. It is generally supposed that this is the case, but it is hard to find any justification for this assumption. It is not easy to see how one might go about answering this question because of unclarities in the notion of a function itself. It is not clear what boundaries there are on what functions exist. Our strategy is to dodge this issue rather than trying to resolve it. Just as in the case of relations, in set theory we confine our attention to functions in extension, distinguishing between them and functions in intension, and we reserve the term 'function' for functions in extension.

The preceding definition is for one-place functions. We can extend it to n-place functions by regarding the latter as one-place functions of ordered n-tuples. To make our notation look more conventional we define:

Def: If f is a function, $f(x) = y$ iff xfy.

Def: If f is an n-place function, $f(x_1,...,x_n) = f(\langle x_1,...,x_n \rangle)$.

4.1 Mappings Into and Onto

Our definitions of 'domain', 'range', and 'field' carry over directly to functions. A function is said to *map* its domain onto its range. If $f(x) = y$, we sometimes say that *f maps x onto y*. More generally, applying the notion of the relational image of a set to the special case in which the relation is a function, we obtain the *functional image of a set*:

Def: If f is a function, $f*A = \{y \mid (\exists x)(x \in A \ \& \ y = f(x)\}$.

A more perspicuous way of writing this definition is:

$$f*A = \{f(x) \mid x \in A\}.$$

$f*A$ is the set of all objects to which f maps elements of A. It can be diagrammed as follows:

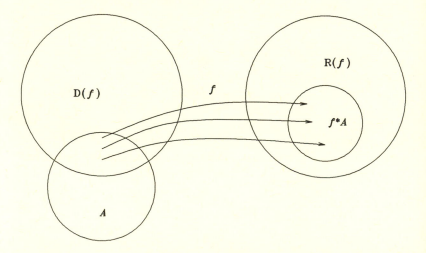

We say that a function maps one set *into* another if the f-image of the first set is a subset of the second set:

Def: $f:A \longrightarrow B$ iff f is a function & $A \subseteq \mathbf{D}(f)$ & $f*A \subseteq B$.

We say that a function maps one set *onto* another if it maps the first set into the second, and the f-image of the first set includes all of the second set:

Def: $f:A \underset{\text{onto}}{\longrightarrow} B$ iff f is a function & $A \subseteq \mathbf{D}(f)$ & $f*A = B$.

For instance, the function $(x+1)$ maps the set ω of natural numbers into itself. But it does not map ω onto itself because 0 is not in the range of this function.

4.2 Operations on Functions

Suppose g maps A onto B, and f maps B onto C:

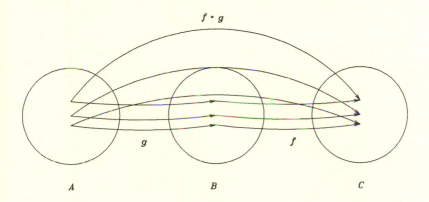

By putting these two mappings together, we get a mapping of A onto C. This is called *the composition of f and g* and is defined as follows:

Def: $f \circ g$ is $\{\langle x,y \rangle \mid x \in \mathbf{D}(g)$ & $y = f(g(x))\}$.

(4.1)   If $x \in \mathbf{D}(f \circ g)$ then $(f \circ g)(x) = f(g(x))$.

Notice that $f \circ g$ is just the relative product f/g.

4.3 The Restriction of a Function

The *restriction* of a function f to a set A is the function that results from restricting the domain of f to A:

Def: $f{\restriction}A = \{\langle x,y\rangle \mid x{\in}A \ \& \ f(x) = y\}$.

For example, if f is the function '$x+1$' on the natural numbers, and **O** is the set of odd numbers, then $f{\restriction}\mathbf{O}$ is the function '$x+1$' defined just for the odd numbers.

Practice exercises:
1. $\mathbf{D}(f{\restriction}A) \subseteq A$.
2. $\mathbf{D}(f{\restriction}A) = A$ iff $A \subseteq \mathbf{D}(f)$.

4.4 One-One Functions

A function maps its domain onto its range. Some functions have the further characteristic that no two elements of their domain are mapped onto the same element of their range. Such functions establish a one-one correspondence between the objects in their domain and the objects in their range and are called *one-one functions*:

Def: f is a one-one function iff f is a function and for each x and y in $\mathbf{D}(f)$, if $x \neq y$ then $f(x) \neq f(y)$.

A function f is also a relation, and f^{-1} is its converse. f^{-1} will not usually be a function, but if f is one-one then it establishes a one-one correspondence between elements of the domain and elements of the range, and hence f^{-1} is also a function. The converse of a one-one function is called its *inverse*. We have the following theorem:

(4.2) f is a one-one function iff both f and f^{-1} are functions.

We introduce the terminology 'f maps A one-one onto (or into) B':

Def: $f{:}A \xrightarrow[\text{onto}]{1-1} B$ iff $f{\restriction}A$ is a one-one function and $f{:}A \xrightarrow[\text{onto}]{} B$.

Def: $f:A \xrightarrow{1-1} B$ iff $f \upharpoonright A$ is a one-one function and $f:A \longrightarrow B$.

Practice exercise: If f is a one-one function and $x \in D(f)$ then $f^{-1}(f(x)) = x$.

4.5 Ordered n-tuples

We defined ordered n-tuples in terms of ordered pairs, stipulating that $\langle x_1,...,x_{n+1} \rangle = \langle \langle x_1,...,x_n \rangle, x_{n+1} \rangle$. There is another common way of defining ordered n-tuples, and that is in terms of functions. Corresponding to each ordered n-tuple $\langle x_1,...,x_n \rangle$ is a function f such that (1) the domain of f is the set of n non-negative integers, $\{0,...,n-1\}$, and (2) for each $i \leq n-1$, $f(i) = x_{i+1}$. f is just a mapping from $\{0,...,n-1\}$ to $\{x_1,...,x_n\}$ where the mapping indicates the ordering of the x_i's in terms of the ordering of the integers corresponding to them. The alternative definition of ordered n-tuples identifies them with these functions, i.e., it sets:

$$\langle x_1,...,x_n \rangle = \{\langle 0,x_1 \rangle,...,\langle n-1,x_n \rangle\}.$$

This is an elegant way of proceeding, and the reader will no doubt encounter it occasionally, but it will not be used in this book. Note that it has one disadvantage. This is that it cannot be used to define 'ordered pair', because the definition requires a prior notion of ordered pairs. Thus ordered pairs must be defined in the standard way, which is then different from the way ordered n-tuples for all $n > 2$ are defined.

4.6 Relational Structures and Isomorphisms

A relational structure is just a set together with a group of relations each having that set as its field. The simplest case is that of a set and a single relation. For instance, $\langle \omega, < \rangle$ is a relational structure consisting of the natural numbers and the ordering relation $<$. The more general case of a relational structure gives us $(n+1)$-tuples of the form $\langle A, R_1,...,R_n \rangle$ where each R_i is a relation whose field is A. A is called 'the field' of the relational structure because it is the field of all the relations in the structure. Relational structures are the subject matter of most mathematical theories, but one should not suppose that they are of significance

only in mathematics. Many philosophical theories can be viewed
as attempts to describe relational structures. For instance, we
might consider a philosophical theory that is about concepts and
their entailment relations. Taking C to be the set of all concepts,
and E to be the relation of entailment between concepts, this
theory could be viewed as being about the relational structure
$\langle C,E \rangle$.

It is generally the abstract form of a relational structure that
is of interest. When two relational structures have the same form,
we say that they are *isomorphic*. More precisely, to say that $\langle A,R_1,...,R_n \rangle$
is isomorphic to $\langle B,S_1,...,S_n \rangle$ is to say that A and B can be put
into a one-one correspondence in such a way that for each of the
R_i's, elements of A stand in R_i to one another iff the corresponding elements of B stand in the corresponding relation S_i to one
another. Such a one-one correspondence is an *isomorphism*. This
is defined as follows:

Def: If $\langle A,R_1,...,R_n \rangle$ and $\langle B,S_1,...,S_n \rangle$ are relational structures,
then $\langle A,R_1,...,R_n \rangle \simeq_f \langle B,S_1,...,S_n \rangle$ iff
(1) f maps A one-one onto B; and
(2)   for each R_i, if R_i is a k-place relation then S_i is also
a k-place relation, and for each k-tuple $\langle x_1,...,x_k \rangle$ of
elements of A, $\langle x_1,...,x_k \rangle \in R_i$ iff $\langle f(x_1),...,f(x_k) \rangle \in S_i$.

An isomorphism maps A one-one onto B in such a way as to
preserve the structure of the relational structures. For example,
if R simple orders A and S simple orders B and we draw A and
B as lines, then if we draw arrows between A and B representing
f, the arrows will not cross (indicating that the ordering is the same
for both A and B):

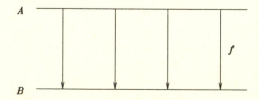

In general, an isomorphism preserves the structure of the relations involved in a relational structure. For instance, we have the following simple theorems:

(4.3)   If $\langle A,R \rangle$ and $\langle B,S \rangle$ are relational structures and $\langle A,R \rangle$ $\approx_f \langle B,S \rangle$, then R is transitive iff S is transitive.

Proof: Suppose $\langle A,R \rangle$ and $\langle B,S \rangle$ are relational structures, $\langle A,R \rangle$ $\approx_f \langle B,S \rangle$, and R is transitive. To show that S is transitive, suppose $x,y,z \in B$ and xSy & ySz. $f(f^{-1}(x)) = x$, $f(f^{-1}(y)) = y$, and $f(f^{-1}(z)) = z$, so $f^{-1}(x)Rf^{-1}(y)$ iff xSy, $f^{-1}(y)Rf^{-1}(z)$ iff ySz, and $f^{-1}(x)Rf^{-1}(z)$ iff xSz. As xSy & ySz, $f^{-1}(x)Rf^{-1}(y)$ & $f^{-1}(y)Rf^{-1}(z)$. R is transitive, so $f^{-1}(x)Rf^{-1}(z)$. But then xSz. So S is transitive.

Obviously, the same style of proof can be used for virtually any property of relations to show that if one relational structure has the property then so does another relational structure isomorphic to the first. In particular,

(4.4)   If $\langle A,R \rangle$ and $\langle B,S \rangle$ are relational structures and $\langle A,R \rangle$ $\approx_f \langle B,S \rangle$, then R is a simple ordering of A iff S is a simple ordering of B.

Proof: exercise

(4.5)   If $\langle A,R \rangle$ and $\langle B,S \rangle$ are relational structures and $\langle A,R \rangle$ $\approx_f \langle B,S \rangle$, then R is a well ordering of A iff S is a well ordering of B.

Proof: exercise

5. Recursive Definitions

A *definition* of a concept uniquely determines what objects exemplify the concept under any possible circumstances. There is more than one way to do this. The most straightforward kind of definition is an *explicit definition*. An explicit definition gives necessary and sufficient conditions for something to exemplify the concept. For example, one might define 'bachelor' by saying that something is a bachelor iff it is an unmarried man. But frequently in logic, mathematics, and technical philosophy, we encounter definitions of another sort. For instance, in the propositional calculus we might define 'formula' by stipulating:

- (i) an atomic formula is a formula;
- (ii) if P is a formula then $\sim P$ is a formula;
- (iii) if P and Q are formulas then $(P \& Q)$ is a formula;
- (iv) nothing is a formula that cannot be obtained by (i)–(iii).

Here we give rules for constructing formulas from a basic set (the atomic formulas) and one another, and then stipulate that something is a formula only if it can be constructed using those rules. This is an example of a *recursive definition*. Recursive definitions *look* circular, because the concept being defined (in this case, 'formula') appears within the definition. One of the triumphs of set theory is that it enables us to see how recursive definitions are to be understood and makes it possible to replace recursive definitions with explicit definitions.

A recursive definition of a set A begins by stipulating that the members of some initial set A_0 are in A. A_0 is the *basis* for the recursive definition. Then it stipulates that anything standing in any of a list of relations $R_1,...,R_k$ to things already in A are themselves in A. Taking R_1 to be an $(n+1)$-place relation, R_2 to be an $(m+1)$-place relation, etc., a recursive definition has the general form:

- (i)   if $x \in A_0$, then $x \in A$;
- (ii$_1$) if $x_1,...,x_n \in A$ and $\langle x_1,...,x_n \rangle R_1 y$, then $y \in A$;
- (ii$_2$) if $x_1,...,x_m \in A$ and $\langle x_1,...,x_m \rangle R_2 y$, then $y \in A$;

$$\cdot$$
$$\cdot$$
$$\cdot$$

- (ii$_k$) if $x_1,...,x_j \in A$ and $\langle x_1,...,x_j \rangle R_k y$, then $y \in A$;
- (iii)   nothing is in A that cannot be obtained by (i)–(ii$_k$).

To illustrate, consider once more the recursive definition of the set of formulas of the propositional calculus. There the basis A_0 is the set of atomic formulas. y stands in the relation R_1 to x iff y is the negation of x, and z stands in the relation R_2 to $\langle x,y \rangle$ iff z is the conjunction of x and y.

Recursive definitions can be explained in terms of the concept of *set-theoretic closure*. A set A is *closed* under a relation R provided everything that is R-related to members of A is also a member of A:

Def: If R is an $(n+1)$-place relation then A is closed under R iff, for any $x_1,...,x_n \in A$, if $\langle x_1,...,x_n \rangle Ry$ then $y \in A$.

In other words, collecting objects R-related to members of A does not give us anything that is not already in A. For example, the set of formulas of the propositional calculus is closed under negation because the negation of any formula is a formula. We say that a set is closed under a class of relations iff it is closed under all the relations in the class:

Def: If K is a class of relations, then A is closed under K iff A is closed under every member of K.

Clause (i) of our schematic recursive definition tells us that A contains all the elements of the basis A_0. Clauses $(ii_1)-(ii_k)$ amount to stipulating that A is closed under the relations $R_1,...,R_k$. Clause (iii) is intended to stipulate that A is the *smallest* set satisfying the other conditions. Such a smallest set is called *the closure* of A_0 under $R_1,...,R_k$. But why should we think there is any such smallest set? Set theory allows us to define the closure explicitly and prove that it is the smallest set containing the basis and closed under $R_1,...,R_k$. The explicit definition of the closure is as follows:

Def: $C_K(A_0) = \bigcap \{X \mid A_0 \subseteq X \ \& \ X \text{ is closed under } K\}$.

It must now be shown that $C_K(A_0)$, so defined, is indeed the smallest set containing A_0 and closed under K. Let

$$M = \{X \mid A_0 \subseteq X \ \& \ X \text{ is closed under } K\}.$$

Then:

(5.1) $\quad A_0 \subseteq C_K(A_0)$.

Proof: $\mathbf{C}_K(A_0) = \bigcap M$. If $X \in M$ then $A_0 \subseteq X$, so by theorem (2.36), $A_0 \subseteq \bigcap M$, i.e., $A_0 \subseteq \mathbf{C}_K(A_0)$.

(5.2) $\mathbf{C}_K(A_0)$ is closed under K.

Proof: Pick any R in K. Suppose R is an $(n+1)$-place relation. We will show that $\mathbf{C}_K(A_0)$ is closed under R. Suppose $x_1,...,x_n \in \mathbf{C}_K(A_0)$ and $\langle x_1,...,x_n \rangle Ry$. Then $x_1,...,x_n \in \bigcap M$, so for each X in M, $x_1,...,x_n \in X$. But each X in M is closed under R, so as $x_1,...,x_n \in X$ and $\langle x_1,...,x_n \rangle Ry$, it follows that $y \in X$. This holds for each X in M, so $y \in \bigcap M$, i.e., $y \in \mathbf{C}_K(A_0)$. Therefore, $\mathbf{C}_K(A_0)$ is closed under every R in K, and hence $\mathbf{C}_K(A_0)$ is closed under K.

(5.3) $\mathbf{C}_K(A_0)$ is the smallest set containing A_0 and closed under K, i.e., if $X \in M$ then $\mathbf{C}_K(A_0) \subseteq X$.

Proof: $\mathbf{C}_K(A_0) = \bigcap M$. If $X \in M$ then $\bigcap M \subseteq X$, so $\mathbf{C}_K(A_0) \subseteq X$.

The concept of the closure of a set under a class of relations makes precise the concept of a recursive definition. A recursive definition can be transformed into an explicit definition by considering the closure of its basis under the relations used in the recursion. For example, we could replace the definition of 'formula of the propositional calculus' given above by the explicit definition:

$$Fm = \bigcap \{X \mid At \subseteq X \ \& \ (\forall p)(p \in X \supset \text{`} {\sim} p\text{'} \in X)$$
$$\& \ (\forall p)(\forall q)(p,q \in X \supset \text{`}(p\&q)\text{'} \in X)\}$$

where At is the set of atomic formulas.

Consider another example of the use of set-theoretic closure to define a complicated concept. Given a relation R, the *ancestral* of R, symbolized R^∞, is intuitively supposed to be

$$R \cup (R/R) \cup (R/R/R) \cup (R/R/R/R) \cup \ ...$$

The name comes from the fact that if R is the relation 'parent of' then R^∞ is the relation 'ancestor of'. That is, $xR^\infty y$ iff either x is a parent of y, or x is a parent of a parent of y, or x is a parent of a parent of a parent of y, or etc. We can give an explicit definition of the ancestral in terms of set-theoretic closure. We first define the set of R-descendants of an object x. This could be done recursively as follows:

(i)   if xRy then y is an R-descendant of x;
(ii) if y is an R-descendant of x and yRz then z is an R-descendant of x;
(iii) nothing is an R-descendant of x that cannot be obtained by (i) and (ii).

This can be turned into an explicit definition. Recall that $R^*\{x\} = \{y \mid xRy\}$. Then define:

Def: $R^\infty\{x\} = \mathbf{C}_{\{R\}}(R^*\{x\})$.

The ancestral of R is then:

Def: $R^\infty = \{\langle x,y \rangle \mid y \in R^\infty\{x\}\}$.

(5.4)   If R is a relation then $R \subsetneq R^\infty$.

Proof: Suppose $\langle x,y \rangle \in R$. Then $y \in R^*\{x\}$. By (5.1), $R^*\{x\} \subseteq R^\infty\{x\}$, so $y \in R^\infty\{x\}$. Thus $\langle x,y \rangle \in R^\infty$.

One of the most important features of set-theoretical closure is that it gives rise to a general principle of mathematical induction. Consider the special case of the closure of a set under a single binary relation: $\mathbf{C}_{\{R\}}(A_0)$. Consider some property P, and suppose we can establish:

(a)   if $x \in A_0$ then x has P;
(b)   if x has P and xRy then y has P.

We can think of the closure as resulting from adding to A_0 everything standing in the relation R to any member of A_0, and then adding everything standing in the relation R to anything in the resulting larger set, and so on indefinitely. Everything in A_0 has P, and anything R-related to something that has P has P, so in constructing $\mathbf{C}_{\{R\}}(A_0)$ we never add anything that does not have the property P. Thus from (a) and (b) it should follow that everything in $\mathbf{C}_{\{R\}}(A_0)$ has the property P. This is the *principle of set-theoretic induction*:

(5.5)   If R is a binary relation and P is a property such that
      (a) if $x{\in}A_0$ then x has P;
      (b) if x has P and xRy then y has P.
     then everything in $\mathbf{C}_{\{R\}}(A_0)$ has P.

Proof: Let $A = \{x \mid x{\in}\mathbf{C}_{\{R\}}(A_0) \ \& \ x$ has $P\}$. By (a), $A_0 \subseteq A$, and by (b), A is closed under R. Therefore, by (5.3), $\mathbf{C}_{\{R\}}(A_0) \subseteq A$, i.e., everything in $\mathbf{C}_{\{R\}}(A_0)$ has P.

Obviously, this principle can be generalized to apply to arbitrary set-theoretic closures (not just closures under a single binary relation). The formulation of the general principle is left as an exercise to the reader.

    The principle of set-theoretic induction is an extremely powerful principle that can be used to prove important theorems about specific sets defined by set-theoretic closure. A proof by set-theoretic induction proceeds in two steps. The first step is what is called the *basis step*. In this step, it is shown that the members of the basis A_0 have the property P. Then in the *induction step*, we suppose that x has P and suppose that xRy, and show that it follows from this that y has P. The supposition that x has P is called *the induction hypothesis*. This terminology is useful as a bookkeeping device for keeping track of where you are in a proof. To illustrate its use, consider a pair of simple theorems proven by set-theoretic induction:

(5.6)   If $x{\in}\mathbf{C}_{\{R\}}(A_0)$ then either $x{\in}A_0$ or for some y in $\mathbf{C}_{\{R\}}(A_0)$, yRx.

Proof: We prove this by set-theoretic induction. For the basis step, we must prove that if $x{\in}A_0$ then either $x{\in}A_0$ or for some y in $\mathbf{C}_{\{R\}}(A_0)$, yRx. But this is a tautology, so the basis step is established. For the induction step, suppose $x{\in}\mathbf{C}_{\{R\}}(A_0)$ (this is the induction hypothesis) and suppose yRx. We must show that $y{\in}\mathbf{C}_{\{R\}}(A_0)$. But this follows immediately from the fact that $\mathbf{C}_{\{R\}}(A_0)$ is closed under R. Thus the induction step is completed, and the theorem follows.

The proof of the following theorem is analogous, and it is left as an exercise to the student:

(5.7)   If $x \in \mathbf{C}_{\{R\}}(A_0)$ then either $x \in A_0$ or $x \in R^*A_0$ or for some y in $\mathbf{C}_{\{R\}}(R^*A_0)$, yRx.

Next, let us use set-theoretic induction to prove a more difficult theorem. The following theorem about ancestrals seems obvious, but it is extremely difficult to prove it without using set-theoretic induction.

(5.8) R^∞ is transitive.

Proof: We want to show that if $xR^\infty y$ and $yR^\infty z$ then $xR^\infty z$, i.e., show that if $y \in R^\infty\{x\}$ and $z \in R^\infty\{y\}$ then $z \in R^\infty\{x\}$. Equivalently, suppose $y \in R^\infty\{x\}$, and prove that for any z, if $z \in R^\infty\{y\}$ then $z \in R^\infty\{x\}$. We do this by set-theoretic induction, recalling that $R^\infty\{y\}$ is $\mathbf{C}_{\{R\}}(R^*\{y\})$. Let P be the property of being a member of $R^\infty\{x\}$.
    For the basis step, suppose $z \in R^*\{y\}$. In other words, yRz. By hypothesis, $y \in R^\infty\{x\}$, and $R^\infty\{x\}$ is closed under R, so $z \in R^\infty\{x\}$, i.e., z has P.
    For the induction step, suppose w has P and wRz. In other words, $w \in R^\infty\{x\}$. $R^\infty\{x\}$ is closed under R, so $z \in R^\infty\{x\}$, i.e., z has P.
    Therefore, $z \in R^\infty\{x\}$, i.e., $\langle x,z \rangle \in R^\infty$.

The following useful theorem brings together several concepts defined in separate contexts:

(5.9)   If $\langle A,R \rangle$ and $\langle B,S \rangle$ are relational structures and $\langle A,R \rangle \simeq_f \langle B,S \rangle$ then $\langle A,R^\infty \rangle \simeq_f \langle B,S^\infty \rangle$.

Proof: Suppose $\langle A,R \rangle \simeq_f \langle B,S \rangle$ and $x,y \in A$. We must show that $xR^\infty y$ iff $f(x)S^\infty f(y)$. Suppose $xR^\infty y$, i.e., $y \in R^\infty\{x\}$. We want to show that $f(y) \in S^\infty\{f(x)\}$. We prove this by set-theoretic induction, letting P be the property of y expressed by '$f(y) \in S^\infty\{f(x)\}$':
    For the basis step, suppose $y \in R^*\{x\}$. Then xRy. As $\langle A,R \rangle \simeq_f \langle B,S \rangle$, $f(x)Sf(y)$. But then $f(y) \in S^*\{f(x)\}$, so $f(y) \in S^\infty\{f(x)\}$, i.e., $f(y)$ has P.

For the induction step, suppose y has P and yRz. Then $f(y) \in S^\infty\{f(x)\}$ and $f(y)Sf(z)$. $S^\infty\{f(x)\}$ is closed under S, so $f(z) \in S^\infty\{f(x)\}$, i.e., $f(z)$ has P.

It follows by set-theoretic induction that every member of $R^\infty\{x\}$ has P. Therefore, $f(y) \in S^\infty\{f(x)\}$. So if $xR^\infty y$ then $f(x)S^\infty f(y)$). The converse is analogous.

Practice exercises:
1. $R/R \subseteq R^\infty$.
2. $(R^\infty)^\infty = R^\infty$.

6. Arithmetic

One of the main reasons that set theory is considered philosophically important is that it provides a foundation for mathematics in the sense that (a) all of the concepts of classical mathematics can be defined within set theory, and (b) all of the theorems of classical mathematics become theorems of set theory given these definitions. It became apparent in the nineteenth century, through the work of such mathematicians as Dedekind and Cauchy, that all of classical mathematics can be constructed on the basis of set theory and the arithmetic of the natural numbers, so what remains is to show that arithmetic can be reduced to set theory.

6.1 Peano's Axioms
The *natural numbers* are the non-negative integers 0,1,2,... . Arithmetic is the theory of the natural numbers. It is commonly alleged that the natural numbers can be defined within set theory. The standard procedure is to define zero to be ø, and then each subsequent natural number is taken to be the set of all its predecessors. Thus:

$$0 = \emptyset$$
$$1 = \{0\} = \{\emptyset\}$$
$$2 = \{0,1\} = \{\emptyset,\{\emptyset\}\}$$
$$3 = \{0,1,2\} = \{\emptyset,\{\emptyset\},\{\emptyset,\{\emptyset\}\}\}$$
$$\text{etc.}$$

This is apt to seem mysterious. Is zero really the empty set? Surely not, any more than the ordered pair $\langle x,y \rangle$ is "really" the set $\{\{x\},\{x,y\}\}$. Rather, what the set theorist is doing is constructing a sequence of sets that "work like the natural numbers". But what is it to work like the natural numbers? That is answered by turning to what are known as *Peano's axioms*. This is a set of axioms that completely characterizes the structure of the natural numbers. They are actually due to Dedekind, who conveyed them to Peano in a letter. Peano explicitly represented them as being due to Dedekind, but in one of the great injustices of intellectual history, they have become known as 'Peano's axioms'. They proceed in terms of the primitive symbols N ('is a natural number'), 0, S (the successor function, i.e., $x+1$), and are as follows:

P1. $N(0)$.

P2. If $N(x)$ then $N(S(x))$ (if x is a number, so is its successor).

P3. $\sim(\exists x)[N(x) \,\&\, 0 = S(x)]$ (0 is not the successor of any number).

P4. If $N(x) \,\&\, N(y)$ and $S(x) = S(y)$ then $x = y$ (if two numbers have the same successor, they are the same number).

P5. If $0 \in X$ and $(\forall x)[$if $N(x) \,\&\, x \in X$ then $S(x) \in X]$, then $(\forall x)(N(x) \supset x \in X)$ (mathematical induction).

P5 is the principle of mathematical induction. Most theorems about natural numbers are proven using mathematical induction. It is useful to reformulate **P5** as follows:

Principle of Mathematical Induction:
   Suppose P is a property such that: (1) 0 has P; and (2) for any natural number n, if n has P then $S(n)$ has P. Then all natural numbers have P.[3]

---

[3] It might be doubted that this is really equivalent to **P5**, on the grounds that there need not be such a set as the set of all things having the property P. But there is never any difficulty about there being such a set as the *set of all natural numbers* having P, and that is all that is required for the equivalence.

Perhaps the simplest way to understand the principle of mathematical induction is to think of the natural numbers as analogous to a row of falling dominoes. Once the first domino tips, each of the rest tips in turn.

A proof by mathematical induction that all natural numbers have some property P proceeds by two steps. The first step is what is called 'the basis step' and consists of a proof that 0 has P. The second step is the 'induction step' and consists of proving that if a number has P so does its successor. It then follows that every natural number has P. In the induction step, we typically proceed by saying, 'Suppose n has P' and then proving that $S(n)$ has P. The supposition that n has P is called 'the induction hypothesis'. This terminology is useful for the purpose of making it clear where we are at any given point in a proof by mathematical induction. This will be illustrated below.

Our previous work on set-theoretic closure enables us to see exactly how Peano's axioms characterize the natural numbers. Intuitively, the natural numbers are what we get when we start with 0 and then keep adding one. In other words, the set of all natural numbers is the closure of {0} under the successor function. The conjunction of three of Peano's axioms turn out to be equivalent to this observation. Let us define:

Def: $\omega = \mathbf{C}_{\{S\}}(\{0\})$.

We will prove that the conjunction of **P1**, **P2**, and **P5** holds iff the natural numbers are the same things as the members of ω. It is best to break this into two separate theorems:

(6.1)   If $(\forall x)(N(x) \equiv x \in \omega)$ then **P1**, **P2**, and **P5** hold.

Proof: Suppose $(\forall x)(N(x) \equiv x \in \omega)$. Then:
(a) $0 \in \omega$, so $N(0)$, i.e., **P1** holds.
(b) ω is closed under S, so if $x \in \omega$ then $S(x) \in \omega$, i.e., **P2** holds.
(c)   Suppose $0 \in X$ and $(\forall x)(\text{if } N(x) \ \& \ x \in X \text{ then } S(x) \in X)$. Let $M = \{Y| \ 0 \in Y \ \& \ Y \text{ is closed under } S\}$. $\omega = \bigcap M$, so if $Y \in M$ then $\omega \subseteq Y$. Let $Y = X \cap \omega$. Then $0 \in Y$. Suppose $x \in Y$. Then $N(x)$ and $x \in X$. It follows from the hypothesis that $S(x) \in X$, and of course $S(x) \in \omega$, so $S(x) \in X \cap \omega$, i.e., $S(x) \in Y$. Therefore, $Y \in M$, and hence $\omega \subseteq Y$. But $Y \subseteq X$, so $\omega \subseteq X$. In other words, $(\forall x)(N(x) \supset x \in X)$. So **P5** holds.

(6.2)   If **P1**, **P2**, and **P5** hold then $(\forall x)(N(x) \equiv x \in \omega)$.

Proof: Suppose **P1**, **P2**, and **P5** hold. $0 \in \omega$ and $(\forall x)(x \in \omega \supset S(x) \in \omega)$, so by **P5**, $(\forall x)(N(x) \supset x \in \omega)$. To prove the converse, we use the principle of set-theoretic induction (theorem (5.5)). Recall that $\omega = C_{\{S\}}(\{0\})$. By **P1**, if $x \in \{0\}$ then $N(0)$. By **P2**, if $N(x)$ and $y = S(x)$ then $N(y)$. Thus by (5.5), $(\forall x)(x \in \omega \supset N(x))$.

The remaining two axioms, **P3** and **P4**, characterize the successor function. The best way to understand this characterization is by considering the relationship between the successor function and 'less than'. If x and y are natural numbers then $x < y$ iff $y = S(x)$ or $y = S(S(x))$ or ... . In other words, we can define 'less than' on the natural numbers as the ancestral of the successor function:

Def: $< = S^\infty$.

Def: $n \leq m$ iff $n < m \lor n = m$.

The import of **P3** and **P4** is then explained by the following theorem:

(6.3)   If **P1**, **P2**, and **P5** hold, then **P3** and **P4** hold iff $<$ strict simple orders ω.

The proof of (6.3) turns out to be rather complicated. In order to prove it, we must first prove some preliminary theorems.
    We begin by noting that $<$ is transitive. This follows immediately from the fact that the ancestral of any relation is transitive:

(6.4) $<$ is transitive.

The following theorem results from spelling out the definition of $<$:

(6.5) $m < n$ iff $n \in C_{\{S\}}(\{S(m)\})$.

Proof: '$m < n$' was defined to mean that $mS^\infty n$. This in turn was defined to mean that $n \in S^\infty\{m\}$, which was in turn defined to mean that $n \in C_{\{S\}}(S^*\{m\})$, i.e., $n \in C_{\{S\}}(\{S(m)\})$.

(6.5) enables us to see that as an immediate consequence of theorem (5.6) we have:

(6.6) $m < n$ iff either $n = S(m)$ or $(\exists y)(m < y \ \& \ n = S(y))$.

Proof: From right to left is easy. $m < S(m)$, so if $S(m) = n$ then $m < n$. On the other hand, suppose there is a y such that $m < y$ and $S(y) = n$. Then we have $m < y < S(y) = n$, so $m < n$. For the converse, recall (5.6), which tells us that:

> If $x \in C_{\{R\}}(A_0)$ then either $x \in A_0$ or $(\exists y)[y \in C_{\{R\}}(A_0) \ \& \ yRx]$.

As an instance of this we have:

> If $n \in C_{\{S\}}(\{S(m)\})$ then either $n \in \{S(m)\}$ or $(\exists y)[y \in C_{\{S\}}(\{S(m)\}) \ \& \ ySn]$.

By (6.5) this is equivalent to:

> If $m < n$ then either $n = S(m)$ or $(\exists y)[m < y \ \& \ S(y) = n]$.

We prove the following theorem in a precisely similar fashion using (5.7) in place of (5.6):

(6.7)   If $m < n$ then either $n = S(m)$ or $n = S(S(m))$ or $(\exists y)[S(m) < y \ \& \ n = S(y)]$.

We have two quick corollaries of (6.6):

(6.8)   If $n \in \omega$ then $n < S(n)$.

(6.9)   If **P3** holds and $x \in \omega$ then $\sim(x < 0)$.

Proof: If $x < y$ then by (6.6), $(\exists z)y = S(z)$, but then by **P3**, $y \neq 0$.

The following theorem is easily proven by mathematical induction using (6.6):

(6.10)   If $n \in \omega$ & $n \neq 0$ then $0 < n$.

Proof: exercise

(6.11)   If $n \in \omega$ then $0 < S(n)$.

Proof by induction.   Details left as an exercise.

(6.12)   If $m < n$ then $S(m) \leq n$.

Proof: Suppose $m < n$.   Then by (6.7), either (a) $n = S(m)$ or (b) $n = S(S(m))$ or (c) $(\exists y)[S(m) < y$ & $n = S(y)]$.   By (6.6), the disjunction of (b) and (c) holds iff $S(m) < n$.

We have observed that $<$ is transitive.   To show that it is a strict simple ordering, it remains to show that it is connected and asymmetric.   Connectedness follows from its definition in terms of set-theoretic closure and does not require the assumption of any of Peano's axioms:

(6.13) $<$ is connected.

Proof: We will prove by set-theoretic induction that for each n in ω, $(\forall m)[m \in \omega \supset (n = m \lor n < m \lor m < n)]$.   By (6.10), if $m \neq 0$ then $0 < m$.   Now suppose that $(\forall m)[m \in \omega \supset (n = m \lor n < m \lor m < n)]$, and let us show that $(\forall m)[m \in \omega \supset (S(n) = m \lor S(n) < m \lor m < S(n))]$.   Suppose $m \in \omega$.   If $n = m$, then $m < S(n)$.   If $m < n$, then as $n < S(n)$, it follows that $m < S(n)$.   Suppose, finally, that $n < m$.   Thus by (6.6), either $m = S(n)$ or for some y such that $n < y$, $m = S(y)$.   In the latter case, by (6.12), $S(n) \leq y < S(y) = m$, so $S(n) < m$.

It is only for the proof of asymmetry that we must assume **P3** and **P4**.   We begin by noting the following consequence of **P4**:

(6.14)   If **P4** holds then $m < S(n) \supset m \leq n$.

Proof: Suppose **P4** holds.   Suppose $m < S(n)$.   Then by (6.6), either $S(n) = S(m)$, and hence by **P4** $m = n$, or for some y such that $m < y$, $S(n) = S(y)$.   In the latter case, by **P4**, $n = y$, and hence $m < n$.

Then we obtain asymmetry as follows:

(6.15)   If **P3** and **P4** hold then < is asymmetric.

Proof: Suppose **P3** and **P4** hold.   We prove by set-theoretic induction that for each n, $(\forall m)[m < n \supset {\sim}(n < m)]$.   For the basis, we observe that by (6.9), ${\sim}(m < 0)$.   For the induction step, suppose that $(\forall m)[m < n \supset {\sim}(n < m)]$, and let us show that $(\forall m)[m < S(n) \supset {\sim}(S(n) < m)]$.   Suppose $m < S(n)$.   By (6.14), either (a) $m < n$, or (b) $m = n$.   Suppose (a).   If $S(n) < m$, then as $n < S(n)$, it follows that $n < m$.   But by the induction hypothesis, ${\sim}(n < m)$.   So (a) does not hold.   Suppose (b).   Then $m = n$, and as $S(n) < m$, $S(n) < n$.   But $n < S(n)$, so by transitivity, $n < n$.   By the induction hypothesis, $n < n \supset {\sim}(n < n)$, so ${\sim}(n < n)$.   So (b) too is impossible.   Therefore, ${\sim}(S(n) < m)$.   So by mathematical induction it follows that for every n, $(\forall m)[m < n \supset {\sim}(n < m)]$.

Note that we have now proven that if **P3** and **P4** hold then < is a strict simple ordering.   This gives us half of (6.3).   To prove the converse we must first prove the following two theorems:

(6.16)   If **P1**, **P2**, and **P5** hold and < is a strict simple ordering then **P3** and **P4** hold.

Proof: Suppose **P1**, **P2**, and **P5** hold and < is a strict simple ordering.   If **P3** failed, then for some n, $0 = S(n)$.   But by (6.11), $0 < S(n)$, and then it would follow that $0 < 0$.   This is impossible if < is a strict simple ordering.   Similarly, suppose **P4** failed.   Then for some n,m, $n \neq m$ but $S(n) = S(m)$.   As $n \neq m$, by connectedness, either $n < m$ or $m < n$.   Suppose $n < m$.   Then by (6.12), $S(n) \leq m$. $m < S(m)$, so $S(n) < S(m)$.   But $S(n) = S(m)$, so $S(n) < S(n)$, which is impossible if < is a strict simple ordering.   Thus **P4** cannot fail.

Having explained the import of Peano's axioms, it remains to show that they completely characterize the structure of the natural numbers.   This can be made precise as the claim that any two relational structures that satisfy Peano's axioms are isomorphic.   Once we have proven this it will follow that no relational structure satisfying the axioms can have any more structure than any other, and hence any formal properties of the natural numbers follow from Peano's axioms. But before we can prove this, we must prove some important theorems about natural numbers.

6.2 Inductive Definitions

What will now be shown is that mathematical induction can be used to justify another kind of definition—one equivalent to recursive definitions. This is best illustrated by considering a simple recursive definition. Suppose we start with a set A_0 and then form its closure under a binary relation R. This could be expressed by the following recursive definition:

(i) if $x \in A_0$ then $x \in A$;
(ii) if $x \in A$ and xRy then $y \in A$;
(iii) nothing is in A unless it can be obtained from (i) and (ii).

One way of capturing the intuitive idea behind such a definition is the following. We start with the set A_0 and then we add everything standing in the relation R to its members. This gives us a set A_1:

$$A_1 = A_0 \cup R^*A_0.$$

We repeat the process, adding to A_1 everything standing in the relation R to its members:

$$A_2 = A_1 \cup R^*A_1.$$

We repeat this process indefinitely, defining in general:

$$AS_{(i)} = A_i \cup R^*A_i.$$

Finally, $A = A_1 \cup A_2 \cup ... \cup A_i \cup ...$. More precisely,

$$A = \bigcup\{A_i \mid i \in \omega\}.$$

Intuitively, this should have the result that $A = C_{\{R\}}(A_0)$, and we will prove below that it does. But first let us focus on the definition of the sets A_i. What we are doing here is, in effect, defining a function f on the natural numbers with the result that $f(i) = A_i$. The function f is defined by stipulating:

(i) $f(0) = A_0$;
(ii) $f(S(i)) = f(i) \cup R*f(i)$.

This is an example of an inductive definition of a function. More generally, we can define a function f inductively by choosing any object a_0 and function g and stipulating:

(i) $f(0) = a_0$;
(ii) $f(S(i)) = g(f(i))$.

Intuitively, these two stipulations should determine a function. (i) tells us the value of f for 0, and then by repeated application of (ii) we get the value of f for any other number. For instance, $f(3) = g(g(g(a_0)))$. The following theorem justifies inductive definitions:

(6.17) For any object a_0 and function g there is a unique function f such that:
(i) $\mathbf{D}(f) = \omega$; and
(ii) $f(0) = a_0$; and
(iii) for each i in ω, $f(S(i)) = g(f(i))$.

In order to prove this theorem we first prove:

(6.18) For any object a_0, function g, and natural number n, there is a unique function f_n such that:
(i) $\mathbf{D}(f_n) = \{i \mid i\in\omega \ \& \ i \leq n\}$; and
(ii) $f_n(0) = a_0$; and
(iii) for each $i < n$, $f_n(S(i)) = g(f_n(i))$.

Proof: We first prove by mathematical induction that for each n there is at least one such function. For the basis step, we prove that there is such a function for 0: $f_0 = \{\langle 0, a_0 \rangle\}$. For the inductive step, suppose there is such a function f_n for n. Then let $f_{S(n)} = f_n \cup \{\langle S(n), g(f_n(n)) \rangle\}$. So there is such a function for $S(n)$. It follows that there is such a function for each natural number.

Next we prove that there is at most one such function for each natural number. Suppose there were two functions, f_n and f^*, satisfying (i)–(iii). We prove by mathematical induction that $(\forall i)($if $i \in \omega$ & $i \leq n$ then $f_n(i) = f^*(i))$. For the basis step, it follows from (i) that $f_n(0) = f^*(0) = a_0$, so this holds for 0. For the induction step, suppose that $f_n(i) = f^*(i)$, and let us show that this holds for $S(i)$ as well. As $f_n(i) = f^*(i)$, by (iii), $f_n(S(i)) = g(f_n(i)) = g(f^*(i)) = f^*(S(i))$. Thus f_n and f^* have the same values everywhere and hence are the same function.

We can now prove (6.17) as follows:

Proof: Let $f = \bigcup \{f_n \mid n \in \omega\}$. To see that this is a function, note that the different f_n's have the same values insofar as their domains overlap. That is, if $n < m$ and $i < n$ then $f_m(i) = f_n(i)$. This is because $f_m \restriction \{j \mid j \leq n\}$ will be a function satisfying (i)–(iii) of (6.18), and we know that there is only one such function. As f is a function, it has the same values as the f_n's, so it satisfies (i)–(iii).

A function f defined by (6.17) is said to be *defined inductively*. We can also give inductive definitions of sets by choosing an initial set A_0 and a function g and stipulating:

$$\text{For each } n, \; A_{S(n)} = g(A_n).$$
$$A = \bigcup \{A_n \mid n \in \omega\}.$$

The effect of this definition is to define a function f such that for each n, $f(n) = A_n$, and then taking $A = \bigcup R(f)$. f is defined inductively by stipulating:

$$f(0) = A_0;$$
$$f(S(n)) = g(f(n)).$$

It was remarked above that definitions by set-theoretic closure can be replaced by inductive definitions. We can now prove this:

(6.19)   If $A = \bigcup \{A_n \mid n \in \omega\}$, where for each n $A_{S(n)} = A_n \cup R^*(A_n)$, then $A = \mathbf{C}_{\{R\}}(A_0)$.

Proof: First we prove by mathematical induction that for each n, $A_n \subseteq \mathbf{C}_{\{R\}}(A_0)$. We know that $A_0 \subseteq \mathbf{C}_{\{R\}}(A_0)$. Suppose that $A_n \subseteq \mathbf{C}_{\{R\}}(A_0)$. Suppose $x \in A_{S(n)}$. Then either $x \in A_n$ (in which case $x \in \mathbf{C}_{\{R\}}(A_0)$), or for some y in A_n, yRx. By hypothesis, $y \in \mathbf{C}_{\{R\}}(A_0)$ and $\mathbf{C}_{\{R\}}(A_0)$ is closed under R, so in the latter case it is also true that $x \in \mathbf{C}_{\{R\}}(A_0)$. Therefore $A_{S(n)} \subseteq \mathbf{C}_{\{R\}}(A_0)$. It follows by mathematical induction that for $\mathbf{C}_{\{R\}}(A_0)$, i.e., $A \subseteq \mathbf{C}_{\{R\}}(A_0)$.

Conversely, we prove by set-theoretic induction that $\mathbf{C}_{\{R\}}(A_0) \subseteq A$. First we note that if $x \in A_0$ then $x \in A$. Now suppose $x \in A$ and xRy. We must show that $y \in A$. As $x \in A$, for some n, $x \in A_n$. But then $y \in A_{S(n)}$, so $y \in A$. Therefore, for every x in $\mathbf{C}_{\{R\}}(A_0)$, $x \in A$. Thus $\mathbf{C}_{\{R\}}(A_0) \subseteq A$.

6.3 The Categoricity of Peano's Axioms

It can now be shown in precisely what sense Peano's axioms completely characterize the structure of the natural numbers. A set of axioms is *categorical* if any two relational structures satisfying the axioms are isomorphic. A categorical set of axioms completely characterizes the structure of the relational structures satisfying them. We will prove that Peano's axioms are categorical. We do this by supposing that we have a relational structure $\langle A,F \rangle$ satisfying Peano's axioms, and then show that it follows from this that $\langle A,F \rangle$ is isomorphic to $\langle \omega,S \rangle$.

(6.20) If F is a function and $\mathbf{D}(F) = A$ and
   (I) $a \in A$;
   (II) $x \in A \supset F(x) \in A$;
   (III) $x \in A \supset F(x) \neq a$;
   (IV)   if $x,y \in A$ & $F(x) = F(y)$ then $x = y$;
   (V)   for any X, if $a \in X$ and $(\forall y)(y \in A \cap X \supset F(y) \in X)$, then $A \subseteq X$;
   then $\langle A,F \rangle$ is isomorphic to $\langle \omega,S \rangle$.

Proof: The intuitive idea behind the proof of this theorem is as follows. Just as in theorem (6.2), it follows from axioms I, II, and V that $A = \mathbf{C}_{\{F\}}(\{a\})$. Thus for each x in A, either $x = a$ or for some y in A, $x = F(y)$. Consequently, A can be diagrammed as follows:

$$a$$
$$F(a)$$
$$F(F(a))$$
.
.
.

By III and IV, this sequence never curves back on itself, so we can put A into a 1-1 correspondence with ω as follows:

$$f$$

$$0 \longrightarrow a$$
$$S(0) \longrightarrow F(a)$$
$$S(S(0)) \longrightarrow F(F(a))$$
.
.
.

This isomorphism f can be defined by induction. It maps 0 onto a, then maps the next number onto the next member of A, and so on. In general, if f maps a number n to a member x of A (i.e., $f(n) = x$), then it should map the next number onto the next member of A, i.e., $f(S(n)) = F(x) = F(f(n))$. These two conditions:

$$f(0) = a$$
$$f(S(n)) = F(f(n))$$

constitute an inductive definition of f.

To give a rigorous proof that f is an isomorphism, we must show that (1) f maps ω 1-1 onto A; and (2) $n = S(m)$ iff $f(n) = F(f(m))$:

(1) To establish that f maps ω 1-1 onto A, we begin by proving that f maps ω onto A, i.e., $A \subseteq f^*\omega$. This is done by using (V) (mathematical induction for A and F). The basis step consists of observing that $a = f(0)$, and hence $a \in f^*\omega$. For the induction

step, suppose $y \in A \cap f^*\omega$. So for some n in ω, $y = f(n)$. Then $F(y)$ = $f(S(n))$, so $F(y) \in f^*\omega$. Thus by (V), $A \subseteq f^*\omega$.

Next we show that f is 1-1. We prove by mathematical induction on n that for every natural number n, $(\forall m)[m < n \supset f(m) \neq f(n)]$. This is vacuously true for 0. Suppose it holds for some number n, and let us show that it holds for $S(n)$ as well. If it did not hold for $S(n)$ then there would be some $m < S(n)$ such that $f(m) = f(S(n)) = F(f(n))$. Either $m = 0$ or for some k, $m = S(k)$. If $m = 0$ then $f(m) = a$, and hence it would follow that $F(f(n)) = a$. This is impossible, by (III), so $m \neq 0$. Thus for some k, $m = S(k)$. Suppose, contrary to the theorem, that $f(m)$ = $f(S(n))$. $f(m) = f(S(k)) = F(f(k))$, so $F(f(k)) = F(f(n))$. Then by (IV), $f(k) = f(n)$. $k < S(k) = m$, so by the induction hypothesis, $f(k) \neq f(n)$, which is a contradiction. Thus contrary to supposition, $f(m) \neq f(S(n))$. Therefore, $(\forall m)[m < S(n) \supset f(m) \neq f(S(n))]$. Hence it follows by mathematical induction that for all natural numbers n and m, if $m < n$ then $f(m) \neq f(n)$. But now if there were two natural numbers m and n such that $f(m) = f(n)$, one of them would be less than the other, and this would contradict what we have just proven. Thus f is 1-1.

(2) We want to prove that $n = S(m)$ iff $f(n) = F(f(m))$. Suppose $n = S(m)$. Then $f(n) = f(S(m)) = F(f(m))$. Conversely, suppose $f(n) = F(f(m))$. $F(f(m)) = f(S(m))$, so $f(n) = f(S(m))$. But f is 1-1, so $n = S(m)$.

6.4 Set-Theoretic Surrogates

As I remarked at the beginning of this section, it is often alleged that set theory provides definitions for number theoretic concepts and in particular that the natural numbers are sets. That is nonsense, but what set theory does do is construct surrogates for the natural numbers that "work like the natural numbers". We are now in a position to understand what the latter means. By the categoricity of Peano's axioms, any two relational structures satisfying those axioms are isomorphic. The natural numbers satisfy those axioms, so if we can also construct sets that satisfy them, then it follows that those sets "work like the natural numbers". So let us see how set-theoretic surrogates for the natural numbers can be constructed. The standard procedure is to define these surrogates as follows:

$$0 = \varnothing$$
$$1 = \{0\}$$
$$2 = \{0,1\}$$
$$3 = \{0,1,2\}$$
$$\cdot$$
$$\cdot$$
$$\cdot$$
$$S(n) = \{0,...,n\}$$

This construction has the consequence that for each n, $n = \{x \mid x < n\}$. Consequently, $S(n) = \{x \mid x < S(n)\} = \{x \mid x \leq n\} = \{x \mid x < n\} \cup \{n\} = n \cup \{n\}$. We take this to constitute our formal definition:

Def: $0 = \varnothing$

Def: $S(n) = n \cup \{n\}$.

Once again, we define $\omega = C_{\{S\}}(\{0\})$ and $< = S^{\infty}$. We want to show that when ω is defined in this way, $\langle \omega, S \rangle$ satisfies Peano's axioms. The theorems we have proven up to this point were proven without making any assumptions about 0 and S, so those theorems apply to this choice of 0 and S as much as to any other. In light of this, we know that **P1**, **P2**, and **P5** hold, and we know that **P3** and **P4** hold provided $<$ is a strict simple ordering. We also know that $<$ is transitive and connected. All that remains is to show that it is asymmetric. In order to establish asymmetry, we must explore the properties of the successor relation defined above.

   S was chosen so that each number is the set of all smaller numbers, i.e., $m = \{n \mid n < m\}$. This is expressed by the following theorem:

(6.21)   If $n,m \in \omega$, $n < m$ iff $n \in m$.

Proof: First we prove that $n < m \supset n \in m$. By (6.5), $n < m$ iff $m \in C_{\{S\}}(\{S(n)\})$. So let us prove by set-theoretic induction that if $m \in C_{\{S\}}(\{S(n)\})$ then $n \in m$. For the basis, suppose $m = S(n)$. Then $m = n \cup \{n\}$, so $n \in m$. For the induction step, suppose $n \in m$ and show that $n \in S(m)$. $S(m) = m \cup \{m\}$, so $m \subseteq S(m)$, and hence as $n \in m$, $n \in S(m)$. Thus in general, $n < m \supset n \in m$.

Conversely, we prove by mathematical induction that for each m, $(\forall n)(n \in m \supset n < m)$. For the basis, we note that $n \notin \emptyset$, so $n \notin 0$. For the induction step, suppose that $(\forall n)(n \in m \supset n < m)$, and let us show that this holds for $S(m)$ as well. Suppose $n \in S(m)$, i.e., $n \in m \cup \{m\}$. Then $n = m$ or $n \in m$. By the induction hypothesis then, $n \leq m$. But $m < S(m)$ and $<$ is transitive, so $n < S(m)$.

Next we prove that $<$ is irreflexive:

(6.22) $n \in \omega \supset n \notin n$.

Proof by induction. Keep in mind that '$\in$' and '$<$' amount to the same thing for the natural numbers. The basis follows from the fact that $\emptyset \notin \emptyset$. Suppose $n \notin n$ and show that $S(n) \notin S(n)$. Suppose instead that $S(n) \in S(n)$. Then $n \cup \{n\} \in n \cup \{n\}$. So either (a) $n \cup \{n\} \in n$ or (b) $n \cup \{n\} \in \{n\}$. Suppose (a). $n \in n \cup \{n\}$, and $<$ is transitive, so by (6.21), $n \in n$, which contradicts the induction hypothesis. So (a) is impossible. Suppose (b). Then $n \cup \{n\} = n$. But again, $n \in n \cup \{n\}$, so it follows that $n \in n$, and this contradicts the induction hypothesis. So neither (a) nor (b) is possible, and hence $S(n) \notin S(n)$.

(6.23)   If $n \in \omega$ then $n \subset S(n)$.

Proof: $n \subseteq n \cup \{n\}$. If $n = n \cup \{n\}$ then $n \in n$, which contradicts (6.22).

We can now see that $<$ has an alternative characterization in terms of the proper subset relation:

(6.24)   If $n, m \in \omega$ then $n < m$ iff $n \subset m$.

Proof: exercise

The proper subset relation is asymmetric, so:

(6.25) $<$ is asymmetric.

It follows that $<$ is a strict simple ordering, and hence **P3** and **P4** hold. These were the only remaining axioms to be established, so:

(6.26) $\langle \omega, S \rangle$ satisfies Peano's axioms.

In light of the categoricity of Peano's axioms, it follows that $\langle \omega, S \rangle$ has precisely the same structure as the "real" natural numbers and successor function. Thus for mathematical purposes we need not distinguish between them.

6.5 Arithmetic

The theory of the natural numbers is concerned as much with the arithmetic operations of addition, multiplication, and exponentiation as it is with the structure of $\langle \omega, S \rangle$ itself. However, it is the structure of $\langle \omega, S \rangle$ that makes it possible to define these operations. They are defined by the following inductive definitions:

$$n+0 = n$$
$$n+S(m) = S(n+m)$$

$$n \cdot 0 = 0$$
$$n \cdot S(m) = (n \cdot m)+n$$

$$n^0 = 1$$
$$n^{S(m)} = n^m \cdot n$$

These are not quite inductive definitions in the sense of subsection (b) because these are two-place functions and inductive definitions were only defined for one-place functions, but this is easily rectified. For each n we can define a one-place function $+_n$ inductively:

$$+_n(0) = n$$
$$+_n(S(m)) = S(+_n(m))$$

This is an inductive definition in the sense of (6.17). Then we define the familiar two-place function of addition by stipulating:

$$n+m = +_n(m).$$

We can treat multiplication and exponentiation analogously.

For each relational structure satisfying Peano's axioms, there are unique functions satisfying the inductive definitions of addition, multiplication, and exponentiation. The question arises whether these functions can differ in interesting ways from relational structure to relational structure. That they cannot is determined by the following theorem (whose proof is omitted):

(6.27)   If $R_1,...,R_n$ and $T_1,...,T_n$ are functions (n possibly being zero) and $\langle \omega,S,T_1,...,T_n \rangle \approx_f \langle A,F,R_1,...,R_n \rangle$, and $a = f(0)$ and G and H are functions defined by induction by stipulating:

$$G(0) = k$$
$$G(S(x)) = T_i(G(x))$$

and

$$H(a) = f(k)$$
$$H(f(x)) = R_i(H(x))$$

then $\langle \omega,S,T_1,...,T_n,G \rangle \approx_f \langle A,F,R_1,...,R_n,H \rangle$.

If $\langle A,F \rangle$ satisfies Peano's axioms then it is isomorphic to $\langle \omega,S \rangle$. Let f be the isomorphism mapping ω onto A. Then by (6.27), if we define inductively:

$$H_x(a) = x$$
$$H_x(f(y)) = f(H_x(x))$$

it follows that for each n, $\langle \omega,S,+_n \rangle \approx_f \langle A,F,H_{f(n)} \rangle$. If we then let $H(x,y) = H_x(y)$, it follows that $\langle \omega,S,+ \rangle \approx_f \langle A,F,H \rangle$. By repeating the process we can define a multiplication function M for $\langle A,F \rangle$ and an exponentiation function E with the result that $\langle \omega,S,+,\cdot,exp \rangle \approx_f \langle A,F,H,M,E \rangle$. So it follows that Peano's axioms together with the inductive definitions for addition, multiplication, and exponentiation completely characterize the arithmetic of the natural numbers. To have a convenient label, I will say that Peano's axioms together with the inductive definitions comprise the axioms of "Peano arithmetic". It is impossible to have one relational structure satisfying these axioms that has structure not possessed by another. Thus the axioms for Peano arithmetic are "complete" in the very strong sense that given any additional axiom describing further potential structural features, either (1) the additional axiom already follows from the axioms for Peano arithmetic, in the sense that every relational structure satisfying the axioms for Peano arithmetic already satisfies the additional axiom, or (2) the additional axiom is inconsistent with the axioms for Peano arithmetic, in the sense that no relational structure can satisfy them all.

Practice exercise: Prove by mathematical induction that if $n \in \omega$ then $0+n = n$. In proving this, assume the two clauses of the inductive definition of addition.

CHAPTER TWO
LOGIC

1. The Predicate Calculus

No doubt the most important technical tool in contemporary logic is the predicate calculus. We used it even to discuss set theory. Conversely, set theory will now be used as a tool for studying the predicate calculus.

1.1 Syntax

Formulas of the predicate calculus are constructed out of individual constants, individual variables, relation symbols, and the *logical constants* '&', 'v', '~', '⊃', '≡', '∀', '∃', '(', ')', and '='. We assume that there are infinitely many individual constants and individual variables. It is common to take just '&', '~', '∃', and '=' as primitive logical constants and then the others can be defined in terms of them:

Def: $(P \lor Q)$ is $\sim(\sim P \ \& \sim Q)$
          $(P \supset Q)$ is $(\sim P \lor Q)$
          $(P \equiv Q)$ is $((P \supset Q) \ \& \ (Q \supset P))$
          $(\forall x)P$ is $\sim(\exists x)\sim P$

If '=' is included as a logical constant then we are studying the *predicate calculus with identity*; otherwise we are studying the predicate calculus simpliciter. First courses in logic usually omit '=', but for most of the purposes for which the predicate calculus is actually used, it is important to have '='. For instance, we formulated set theory within the predicate calculus, and it was essential that we had '=' for that purpose.

A relation symbol R has a fixed number of argument places and is used to symbolize relations with that number of places. For instance, a two-place relation symbol is used to symbolize binary relations. A 0-place relation symbol is a *sentence letter*, and a 1-place relation symbol is a *predicate letter*.

The individual constants and individual variables are taken jointly to comprise the *individual symbols*.

An *expression* is any finite string of symbols. Expressions built out of the primitive symbols of the predicate calculus comprise the *object language*. The language we use to talk about the object language, in this case English, is the *metalanguage*. Within the metalanguage we can form a name of an expression of the object language by enclosing that expression in single quotes. Thus

$$'(P \ \& \ Q)'$$

is a name, in the metalanguage, of the object language expression

$$(P \ \& \ Q).$$

In describing how formulas are built, we find ourselves wanting to write things like the following:

(1.1)   If P and Q are formulas, so is '$(P \ \& \ Q)$'.

But this does not mean what we want it to mean. The difficulty is that you cannot quantify into quotation marks, because enclosing an expression containing variables within quotation marks gives us a name of that expression, variables and all. Thus, if A and B are expressions, the following is not an instance of (1.1):

(1.2)   If A and B are formulas, so is '$(A \ \& \ B)$'.

Instead, the corresponding instance of (1.1) is:

If A and B are formulas, so is '$(P \ \& \ Q)$'.

This is not what we want. We must replace (1.1) by something that does have (1.2) as an instance, and for this purpose we want a different kind of quotation mark—one into which we can quantify. For this purpose we use what are called *quasi-quotes* or *corner quotes* and write:

(1.3)   If P and Q are formulas, so is $\ulcorner(P \ \& \ Q)\urcorner$.

The best way to understand corner quotes is as follows. First, (1.3) is a quantificational sentence of the metalanguage, and P and Q are variables of the metalanguage—*metalinguistic variables*. Metalinguistic variables are taken to range over expressions of the object language. We then adopt the convention that enclosing within corner quotes a string of symbols some of which are object language symbols and some of which are metalinguistic variables gives us the name of a *function*, namely, that function which, to each assignment of object language expressions to the metalinguistic variables, assigns the object language expression that results from replacing the metalinguistic variables by those object language expressions. For example, where 'P' and 'Q' are metalinguistic variables, $\ulcorner(P \ \& \ Q)\urcorner$ is that function which, to each pair of object language expressions, assigns their conjunction. In the limiting case in which the string of symbols enclosed by corner quotes contains no metalinguistic variables, we take the corner quotes to work like ordinary single quotes.

The preceding may seem complicated, but the upshot of it is simple. Corner quotes are just quotation marks into which you can quantify, thus legitimizing sentences like (1.3).

The set of formulas of the predicate calculus is defined recursively. We begin by defining the set of *atomic formulas* as follows:

Def: P is an atomic formula iff either:
   (a) P is a sentence letter; or
   (b)   there are individual symbols x and y such that P is $\ulcorner x = y \urcorner$; or
   (c)   there is a relation symbol R with some number of argument places n and there are individual symbols $x_1,...,x_n$ such that P is $\ulcorner Rx_1...x_n \urcorner$.

The recursive definition of the set of formulas is then:

Def: (a)   An atomic formula is a formula;
   (b)   if P is a formula so is $\ulcorner \sim P \urcorner$;
   (c)   if P and Q are formulas so is $\ulcorner(P \ \& \ Q)\urcorner$;
   (d)   if x is an individual variable and P is a formula then $\ulcorner(\exists x)P\urcorner$ is a formula.

This could of course be replaced by an explicit definition in terms of set-theoretic closure. We allow ourselves to replace '(' and ')' by '[' and ']' in the interest of readability.

When a formula is constructed in accordance with clause (d) of the preceding definition, P is said to be the *scope* of the quantifier $\ulcorner(\exists x)\urcorner$. If $\ulcorner(\exists x)P\urcorner$ is then embedded in a longer formula, e.g., in $\ulcorner(R \supset (\exists x)P\urcorner$, the scope of the quantifier remains the same. Thus, for example, in

(1.4) $(\exists x)[Hx \;\&\; \sim(\exists y)(\exists x)Rxy]$

the scope of the first occurrence of '$(\exists x)$' is '$[Hx \;\&\; \sim(\exists y)(\exists x)Rxy]$', the scope of '$(\exists y)$' is '$(\exists x)Rxy$', and the scope of the second occurrence of '$(\exists x)$' is 'Rxy'.

An occurrence of a variable is *bound* by the innermost quantifier containing that same variable within whose scope the occurrence lies. Thus in (1.4), the occurrence of x in 'Hx' is bound by the first '$(\exists x)$' and the occurrence of x in 'Rxy' is bound by the second '$(\exists x)$'. Occurrences of variables within quantifiers are bound by those quantifiers. If an occurrence of a variable is not bound by any quantifier, it is *free*.

If a formula contains no free occurrences of variables, it is a *closed formula*. Otherwise it is an *open formula*. If an open formula contains free occurrences of n different variables, it is an *n-formula*. For instance, 'Rxy' is a two-formula, whereas '$(\forall x)(\forall y)Rxy$' is a closed formula. If a quantifier does not bind any occurrences of variables, it is a *vacuous quantifier*. For instance, the first '$(\forall x)$' is a vacuous quantifier in '$(\forall x)(\forall y)(Fy \supset (\forall x)Gx)$'. It would be more natural to construct the definition of 'formula' in such a way that vacuous quantifiers are prohibited, but that would require us to make all of our definitions more complicated and it would in the end be more trouble than it is worth.

We frequently want to talk about the result of substituting individual symbols for one another in a formula. For example, we want to say that for any P, $\ulcorner(\forall x)P\urcorner$ implies any formula that results from substituting an individual constant for all free occurrences of x in P. Where $x_1,...,x_n$ and $y_1,...,y_n$ are lists of individual symbols, and no two of the x_i's are the same, we let

$$Sb\binom{y_1,\dots,y_n}{x_1,\dots,x_n}P$$

be the result of simultaneously substituting each y_i for all occurrences of x_i in P if x_i is an individual constant and for all free occurrences of x_i in P if x_i is an individual variable. Thus, for example,

$$Sb\binom{y_1,y_2,y_3,d,e}{x_1,x_2,x_3,a,b}(\forall x_1)[Fx_1x_2 \supset Gabx_3]$$

is

$$(\forall x_1)[Fx_1y_2 \supset Gdey_3].$$

No occurrences of 'x_1' get changed in this example because they are all bound.

It is convenient to have a more compact way of writing simple substitutions. I will let $Sb(y/x)P$ be

$$Sb\binom{y}{x}P$$

More generally, we will write $Sb(y_1,\dots,y_n/x_1,\dots,x_n)P$.

1.2 Formal Semantics

We have constructed an artificial symbolism—the "language" of the predicate calculus—by describing its syntax. Next we must describe how this symbolism is to be interpreted. That is accomplished by defining the notion of a *model* and *truth in a model*. We specify a model by specifying a *domain* and specifying the extensions of relation symbols in that domain and the denotations of individual constants. The domain is supposed to consist of all the things we are talking about. The quantifiers are taken to range over the elements of the domain. Formally, we can regard a model as being an ordered pair $\langle D, \mu \rangle$ where D is any non-empty set of objects and μ is a function that assigns to each relation symbol an extension in D and assigns to each individual constant a denotation in D. Precisely:

Def: $\langle D, \mu \rangle$ is a model iff D is a non-empty set and

      (a)   for each sentence letter P, $\mu(P)$ is either 0 or 1 (representing truth values);

      (b)   for each n-ary relation symbol R, $\mu(R)$ is a set of ordered n-tuples of members of D (the extension of R);

      (c)   for each individual constant c, $\mu(c)$ is a member of D (the denotation of c).

A function satisfying (a)–(c) is an *assignment* with respect to D. Thus a model consists of a domain and an assignment with respect to that domain.

    Next we want to give a recursive definition of the notion of truth in a model. This is a bit complicated because only closed formulas have truth values. Open formulas can be regarded as symbolizing relations rather than propositions. Only closed formulas symbolize propositions, so only closed formulas should be assigned truth values in a model. We begin by defining truth for atomic formulas. In the case of sentence letters, a model gives the truth value directly:

Def: If P is a sentence letter, P is true in $\langle D, \mu \rangle$ iff $\mu(P) = 1$.

The definition is equally obvious for identity formulas:

Def: If a and b are individual constants, $\ulcorner a = b \urcorner$ is true in $\langle D, \mu \rangle$ iff $\mu(a) = \mu(b)$, i.e., iff a and b denote the same object in $\langle D, \mu \rangle$.

If R is an n-ary relation symbol and $c_1, ..., c_n$ are individual constants, $\ulcorner Rc_1...c_n \urcorner$ should be true just in case the n-tuples consisting of the denotations of $c_1, ..., c_n$ is in the extension of R, i.e.,

Def: $\ulcorner Rc_1, ..., c_n \urcorner$ is true in $\langle D, \mu \rangle$ iff $\langle \mu(c_1), ..., \mu(c_n) \rangle \in \mu(R)$.

We then define truth for non-atomic formulas recursively:

Def: Recursive definition of truth in $\langle D, \mu \rangle$:
   (a) $\ulcorner \sim P \urcorner$ is true in $\langle D, \mu \rangle$ iff P is false in $\langle D, \mu \rangle$;
   (b) $\ulcorner (P \ \& \ Q) \urcorner$ is true in $\langle D, \mu \rangle$ iff P and Q are both true in $\langle D, \mu \rangle$;
   (c) $\ulcorner (\exists x) P \urcorner$ is true in $\langle D, \mu \rangle$ iff there is some individual constant a not occurring in P and there is an assignment σ that is just like μ except possibly for what it assigns to a, and $Sb(a/x)P$ is true in $\langle D, \sigma \rangle$.

Clause (c) is explained as follows. Suppose first that everything in D has a name. Then $\ulcorner (\exists x) P \urcorner$ is true just in case there is individual constant a such that $Sb(a/x)P$ is true. On the other hand, if not everything in D has a name, then $\ulcorner (\exists x) P \urcorner$ should be true just in case there is some object α in D that can be assigned to some constant a, thereby giving α a name and producing a true substitution instance of P. Because a already denotes something else in μ, this involves modifying μ to construct σ.

To illustrate this definition, consider a simple model in which $D = \{1,2\}$ and $\mu(R) = \{\langle 1,2 \rangle, \langle 2,1 \rangle\}$. Suppose we want to compute the truth value of $\ulcorner (\exists x) Rxx \urcorner$ in $\langle D, \mu \rangle$. We choose a constant that does not occur in $\ulcorner (\exists x) Rxx \urcorner$, for instance, '$a$', and look at $\ulcorner Raa \urcorner$. $\ulcorner (\exists x) Rxx \urcorner$ is true in $\langle D, \mu \rangle$ iff $\ulcorner Raa \urcorner$ is true in some $\langle D, \sigma \rangle$ that is just like $\langle D, \mu \rangle$ except possibly for what it assigns to 'a'. The only possible assignments to 'a' are the numbers 1 and 2. Neither $\langle 1,1 \rangle$ nor $\langle 2,2 \rangle$ is in $\mu(R)$, so it is impossible to make $\ulcorner Raa \urcorner$ true by modifying the assignment to 'a'. Accordingly, $\ulcorner (\exists x) Rxx \urcorner$ is false in $\langle D, \mu \rangle$.

Practice exercises: Compute the truth values of the following closed formulas in the preceding model:
1. $(\forall x)(\exists y) Rxy$
2. $(\exists y)(\forall x) Rxy$
3. $(\forall x)[(\exists y) Rxy \supset (\exists y) Ryx]$

Open formulas symbolize relations rather than propositions, so they do not have truth values in models. Instead, they have extensions. The extension of an n-formula in a model consists of the set of all n-tuples *satisfying* the n-formula in the model. Satisfaction can be defined in terms of truth as follows:

Def: If P is an n-formula whose free variables are $x_1,...,x_n$ (listed in some fixed order), and $a_1,...,a_n$ are individual constants not occurring in P, and $\alpha_1,...,\alpha_n$ are members of D, and σ is an assignment just like μ except that for each i it assigns α_i to a_i, then $\langle\alpha_1,...,\alpha_n\rangle$ *satisfies* P in $\langle D,\mu\rangle$ iff $Sb(a_1,...,a_n/x_1,...,x_n)P$ is true in $\langle D,\sigma\rangle$.

Def: If P is an n-formula, the *extension* of P in $\langle D,\mu\rangle$ is the set of all n-tuples satisfying P in $\langle D,\mu\rangle$.

To illustrate, suppose again that $D = \{1,2\}$ and $\mu(R) = \{\langle1,2\rangle,\langle2,1\rangle\}$, and consider the formula ⌜$(\exists x)Rxy$⌝. An object α satisfies this formula iff assigning α to the constant 'a' makes ⌜$(\exists x)Rxa$⌝ true. Either 1 or 2 can be assigned to 'a', and in either case ⌜$(\exists x)Rxa$⌝ is true. Accordingly, the extension of ⌜$(\exists x)Rxy$⌝ in $\langle D,\mu\rangle$ is $\{1,2\}$.

If a closed formula P is true in $\langle D,\mu\rangle$ we say that $\langle D,\mu\rangle$ is a *model of P*. More generally, if every member of a set Γ of closed formulas is true in $\langle D,\mu\rangle$, we say that $\langle D,\mu\rangle$ is a model of Γ. A closed formula is *satisfiable* iff it has a model. Similarly, a set of closed formulas is satisfiable iff it has a model. A closed formula is *valid* iff it is true in every model. Obviously,

(1.5)   A closed formula is valid iff its negation is unsatisfiable.

Proof: exercise

Practice exercise: Show that ⌜$(\exists x)(Fx \supset (\forall y)Fy)$⌝ is valid.

We say that a closed formula P *implies* a closed formula Q iff every model of P is a model of Q. Similarly, a set Γ of closed formulas implies Q iff every model of Γ is a model of Q.

(1.6) P implies Q iff ⌜$(P \supset Q)$⌝ is valid.

Two closed formulas are *equivalent* iff each implies the other, i.e., iff they have the same models.

We symbolize validity and implication using the turnstile:

Def: $P \models Q$ iff P implies Q.
     $\models P$ iff P is valid.

The rationale for the dual use of the turnstile is provided by the following theorem:

(1.7) $\models P$ iff $\emptyset \models P$.

Proof: exercise

Implication and equivalence have been defined only for closed formulas.   Implication only makes sense for closed formulas because it has to do with truth values, but a notion of equivalence can also be defined for open formulas.   Two n-formulas are equivalent just in case they contain free occurrences of the same variables and have the same extensions in every model:

Def: If P and Q are n-formulas, P and Q are *equivalent* iff they contain free occurrences of the same variables, and for every model $\langle D,\mu \rangle$, the extension of P in $\langle D,\mu \rangle$ is the same as the extension of Q in $\langle D,\mu \rangle$.

Bearing in mind the way in which satisfaction is defined, this is equivalent to requiring:

(1.8)   If P and Q are n-formulas ($n > 0$) and they contain free occurrences of the same variables $x_1,...,x_n$, and $a_1,...,a_n$ are individual constants not occurring in P and Q, then P and Q are equivalent iff $Sb(a_1,...,a_n/x_1,...,x_n)P$ is equivalent to $Sb(a_1,...,a_n/x_1,...,x_n)Q$.

The main significance of equivalence for open formulas is that the *Principle of Replacement* holds:

(1.9)   If P and Q are equivalent formulas, and P occurs within a larger formula R and S results from replacing an occurrence of P by Q in R, then R is equivalent to S.

For instance, because $\ulcorner(Fx \ \& \ Gy)\urcorner$ is equivalent to $\ulcorner(Gy \ \& \ Fx)\urcorner$, it follows that $\ulcorner(\exists x)(\exists y)(Fx \ \& \ Gy)\urcorner$ is equivalent to $\ulcorner(\exists x)(\exists y)(Gy \ \& \ Fx)\urcorner$.

We use the following lemmas to prove the principle of replacement:

(1.10) If P is equivalent to Q then $\sim P$ is equivalent to $\sim Q$.

(1.11) If P is equivalent to Q then $\ulcorner(P \ \& \ R)\urcorner$ is equivalent to $\ulcorner(Q \ \& \ R)\urcorner$ and $\ulcorner(R \ \& \ Q)\urcorner$ is equivalent to $\ulcorner(R \ \& \ P)\urcorner$.

(1.12) If P is equivalent to Q then $\ulcorner(\exists x)P\urcorner$ is equivalent to $\ulcorner(\exists x)Q\urcorner$.

The proof of these lemmas is left as an exercise for the student. The proof of the principle of replacement is then by mathematical induction on the length of a formula. This means that we prove by mathematical induction that for every natural number n, the theorem holds for all formulas of length less than or equal to n, and conclude from that that it holds for all formulas. The basis step is vacuous as there are no formulas of length less than or equal to zero. Suppose then that the principle of replacement holds for all formulas of length less than or equal to n, and let us show that it holds for all formulas of length less than or equal to $n+1$. For this, we need only consider formulas of length exactly $n+1$. We have four possibilities to consider:

(a) Suppose R is atomic. Atomic formulas cannot contain other formulas as parts, so P and R must be the same thing, and hence Q and S must be the same thing. Then as P is equivalent to Q, R is equivalent to S.

(b) Suppose R is a negation, i.e., for some T, $R = \ulcorner\sim T\urcorner$. Then P is a part of T. Then there is a U such that $S = \ulcorner\sim U\urcorner$ and U results from replacing P in T by S. By the induction hypothesis, T is equivalent to U, so by (1.10), R is equivalent to S.

(c) Suppose R is a conjunction $\ulcorner(T \ \& \ U)\urcorner$. Then either P occurs in T or it occurs in U. Suppose the former, the latter case being analogous. Then there is a V such that S is $\ulcorner(V \ \& \ U)\urcorner$ and V results from replacing the occurrence of P in T by Q. By the induction hypothesis, T is equivalent to V, so by (1.11), R is equivalent to S.

(d) Suppose R is $\ulcorner(\exists x)T\urcorner$. This is analogous to the other cases, using theorem (1.12).

A formula is in *prenex normal form* iff it has the form $(Q_1 x_1)...(Q_n x_n)P$ where each Q_i is either a universal or an existential quantifier and P contains no quantifiers. A useful fact about the predicate calculus will be that every closed formula is equivalent to a formula in prenex normal form. This follows from the fact that the following equivalences hold:

(1.13)   If y is a variable that does not occur in either P or Q then:
   (1) $((\forall x)P \mathbin{\&} Q)$ is equivalent to $(\forall y)(Sb(y/x)P \mathbin{\&} Q)$;
   (2) $((\exists x)P \mathbin{\&} Q)$ is equivalent to $(\exists y)(Sb(y/x)P \mathbin{\&} Q)$;
   (3) $(P \mathbin{\&} (\forall x)Q)$ is equivalent to $(\forall y)(P \mathbin{\&} Sb(y/x)Q)$;
   (4) $(P \mathbin{\&} (\exists x)Q)$ is equivalent to $(\exists y)(P \mathbin{\&} Sb(y/x)Q)$;
   (5) $\sim(\forall x)P$ is equivalent to $(\exists x)\sim P$;
   (6) $\sim(\exists x)P$ is equivalent to $(\forall x)\sim P$.

By repeated use of these equivalences we can systematically drive the quantifiers out to the beginning of any formula, thus converting it to prenex normal form. For instance, we can convert $\ulcorner\sim(\exists x)(Fx \mathbin{\&} (\exists x)Gx)\urcorner$ into prenex normal form as follows:

$$\sim(\exists x)(Fx \mathbin{\&} (\exists x)Gx)$$
$$(\forall x)\sim(Fx \mathbin{\&} (\exists x)Gx)$$
$$(\forall x)\sim(\exists z)(Fx \mathbin{\&} Gz)$$
$$(\forall x)(\forall z)\sim(Fx \mathbin{\&} Gz).$$

To actually prove that every formula is equivalent to a formula in prenex normal form, we would use mathematical induction on the length of a formula. That is, we would prove by induction that for every n, if a formula consists of n or fewer primitive symbols then it is equivalent to a formula in prenex normal form.

1.3 Derivations

Derivations are formalized proofs, constructed according to explicit rules proceeding from a fixed list of rules of inference and a fixed list of axioms. In its simplest form we can think of a derivation as a finite string of ordered pairs $\langle\Gamma,P\rangle$ where Γ is a set of closed formulas and P is a closed formula. Each such pair is a "line" of the derivation, and its inclusion in a derivation is to be interpreted as asserting that Γ implies P. In light of this intended interpretation, it is more perspicuous to write the lines in the form '$\Gamma \models P$' rather than '$\langle\Gamma,P\rangle$'. Rules of inference are rules telling us when it is permissible to start a derivation with a given line or to add a given line to a derivation already constructed. Bearing in mind that a derivation is a finite sequence of ordered pairs, the general form of a rule of inference is:

> If σ is a derivation and $\langle \Gamma, P \rangle$ stands in the relation R to σ then the finite sequence resulting from adding $\langle \Gamma, P \rangle$ to the end of σ is also a derivation.

For instance, a simple rule of inference for conjunction has the following form:

(KI) If σ is a derivation and $\langle \Gamma, P \rangle$ and $\langle \Lambda, Q \rangle$ occur in σ then the result of adding $\langle \Gamma \cup \Lambda, (P \& Q) \rangle$ to the end of σ is also a derivation.

This is just the rule that corresponds to the following semantical principle:

> If $\Gamma \models P$ and $\Lambda \models Q$ then $\Gamma \cup \Lambda \models (P \& Q)$.

Thus what **(KI)** amounts to is a rule telling us that if we have already proven that $\Gamma \models P$ and $\Lambda \models Q$ then we can infer that $\Gamma \cup \Lambda \models (P \& Q)$.

Most rules are like **(KI)** in that they tell us that if a derivation already contains certain lines then we can add appropriately related lines. But we must also have rules of inference that allow us to get started by introducing the first line of a derivation. One such rule is the rule of *premise introduction*:

(P) If σ is either $\emptyset$ (i.e., the empty sequence) or a derivation and $P \in \Gamma$ then the result of adding $\langle \Gamma, P \rangle$ to the end of σ is a derivation.

This rule amounts to the observation that a set of formulas implies each of its members. Introducing a premise into a derivation amounts to using this rule.

Another kind of rule that allows us to get started on the first line of a derivation is a rule allowing us to write down an *axiom*. Axioms correspond to rules of the form:

> If σ is either ∅ or a derivation then the result of adding ⟨∅,P⟩
> to the end of σ is a derivation.

Using this rule amounts to asserting P as following from the empty
set, i.e., as being valid. For instance, it will be convenient to have
the following rule of *identity introduction*:

(=I)   If σ is either ∅ or a derivation and c is an individual
         constant then the result of adding ⟨∅,⌜c = c⌝⟩ to the end
         of σ is a derivation.

The following is an example of a derivation:

$$\langle\{P\},P\rangle \qquad\qquad \textbf{(P)}$$
$$\langle\{Q\},Q\rangle \qquad\qquad \textbf{(P)}$$
$$\langle\{P,Q\},(P\ \&\ Q)\rangle \quad \textbf{(KI)}$$

This could be written more perspicuously as follows:

$$\{P\} \vDash P$$
$$\{Q\} \vDash Q$$
$$\{P,Q\} \vDash (P\ \&\ Q).$$

This is the same derivation that might be written in a more
conventional format something like the following:

$$1 \qquad (1) \qquad P$$
$$2 \qquad (2) \qquad Q$$
$$1,2 \qquad (3) \qquad (P\ \&\ Q)$$

In this sort of format we keep track of the premises upon which
a line depends by writing *premise numbers* to the left of each line
number. The effect of this is the same as simply listing the
premises on the left side of each line. Hence each line amounts
to a claim that the premises listed on the left imply the formula
on the right, which is just what our more explicit formulation tells
us.

Given a set of rules of inference, we can define a derivation
(relative to that set of rules) to be any finite set of ordered pairs
⟨Γ,P⟩ that can be constructed using the rules of inference. We say

that P is *derivable from* Γ, and write '$\Gamma \vdash P$', just in case there is a derivation containing $\langle \Gamma, P \rangle$ as a line. Note the difference between '$\vdash$' and '$\models$'. We say that P is a *theorem,* and write '$\vdash P$', just in case $\emptyset \vdash P$. A set of closed formulas is *consistent* iff no contradiction (i.e., formula of the form $\ulcorner (P \,\&\, {\sim}P) \urcorner$) is derivable from it.

A rule like **(KI)** is generally written more perspicuously as follows:

$$\frac{\Gamma \vdash P \qquad \Lambda \vdash Q}{\Gamma \cup \Lambda \vdash (P \,\&\, Q)}$$

The following is a rather standard set of rules of inference for the predicate calculus. Notice that for each logical constant there is an "introduction rule" and an "elimination rule":

(P)
$$\frac{-}{\Gamma \vdash P} \qquad\qquad \text{(provided } P \in \Gamma)$$

(KI)
$$\frac{\Gamma \vdash P \qquad \Lambda \vdash Q}{\Gamma \cup \Lambda \vdash (P \,\&\, Q)} \qquad\qquad (adjunctivity)$$

(KE)
$$\frac{\Gamma \vdash (P \,\&\, Q)}{\Gamma \vdash P} \qquad \frac{\Gamma \vdash (P \,\&\, Q)}{\Gamma \vdash Q} \qquad (simplification)$$

(NI)
$$\frac{\Gamma \vdash P}{\Gamma \vdash {\sim}{\sim}P} \qquad\qquad (double\ negation)$$

(NE)
$$\frac{\Gamma \cup \{{\sim}P\} \vdash (Q \,\&\, {\sim}Q)}{\Gamma \vdash P} \qquad (reductio\ ad\ absurdum)$$

(=I)
$$\frac{-}{\emptyset \vdash c = c} \qquad\qquad (reflexivity\ of\ identity)$$

(=E) $\Gamma \vdash c = d$ $\Lambda \vdash Sb(c/d)P$ (*substitutivity*)
          _____
          $\Gamma \cup \Lambda \vdash P$

(EI) $\Gamma \vdash Sb(a/x)P$ (*existential generalization*)
          _____
          $\Gamma \vdash (\exists x)P$

(EE) $\Gamma \cup \{P\} \vdash Q$ (*existential specification*)
          _____   (provided a does not
          $\Gamma \cup \{(\exists x)Sb(x/a)P\} \vdash Q$ occur in Q or in
                                                  any member of Γ).

Let us call these the *rules for PC-derivations*, and derivations constructed using these rules will be *PC-derivations*. More formally, a PC-derivation is a finite sequence of pairs $\langle \Gamma, P \rangle$ such that each member of the sequence can be added the preceding subsequence in accordance with some rule for PC-derivations. This is a very parsimonious set of rules. The paucity of rules makes PC-derivations difficult to construct. No one in his right mind would use PC-derivations as a tool for proving theorems, but it can be shown that anything derivable from more familiar sets of rules is derivable from these rules. For instance, suppose we want to show that modus ponens holds, i.e., that $\{P, (P \supset Q)\} \vdash Q$. In primitive notation this means that $\{P, \sim(\sim\sim P \ \& \ \sim Q)\} \vdash Q$. This can be established by the following derivation:

$P, \sim Q, \sim(\sim\sim P \ \& \ \sim Q) \vdash P$ (**P**)
$P, \sim Q, \sim(\sim\sim P \ \& \ \sim Q) \vdash \sim\sim P$ (**NI**)
$P, \sim Q, \sim(\sim\sim P \ \& \ \sim Q) \vdash \sim Q$ (**P**)
$P, \sim Q, \sim(\sim\sim P \ \& \ \sim Q) \vdash (\sim\sim P \ \& \ \sim Q)$ (**KI**)
$P, \sim Q, \sim(\sim\sim P \ \& \ \sim Q) \vdash \sim(\sim\sim P \ \& \ \sim Q)$ (**P**)
$P, \sim Q, \sim(\sim\sim P \ \& \ \sim Q) \vdash [(\sim\sim P \ \& \ \sim Q) \ \& \ \sim(\sim\sim P \ \& \ \sim Q)]$ (**KI**)
$P, \sim(\sim\sim P \ \& \ \sim Q) \vdash Q$ (**NE**)

Henceforth I will simply assume without proof that we can derive any particular valid formulas we need with this set of rules of inference. In each case that can be established by actually constructing the appropriate derivation, and the skeptic is invited to do so.

Practice exercises: Construct PC-derivations for the following:
1. $(P \supset Q) \vdash (\sim Q \supset \sim P)$
2. $(\forall x)Fx \vdash Fa$

For PC-derivations we have:

(1.14) A formula is a theorem iff its negation is inconsistent.

Proof: Suppose P is a theorem. Then there is a derivation σ whose last line is $\langle \emptyset, P \rangle$. By adding the following lines to the end of σ we obtain a derivation of $\langle \sim P, (P \ \& \ \sim P) \rangle$:

$$\sim P \ \big| \ \sim P \qquad\qquad \textbf{(P)}$$
$$\sim P \ \big| \ (P \ \& \ \sim P) \qquad\qquad \textbf{(KI)}$$

Conversely, suppose $\sim P$ is inconsistent. Then $\sim P \vdash (Q \ \& \ \sim Q)$, so by **(NE)**, $\emptyset \vdash P$.

For an adequate system of derivations, we should be able to prove all and only valid formulas. To this end we define:

Def: A system of derivations is *sound* iff every theorem is valid, and it is *complete* iff every valid formula is a theorem.

Somewhat stronger notions of soundness and completeness pertain to implication:

Def: A system of derivations is *strongly sound* iff for every set Γ of closed formulas and every closed formula P, if $\Gamma \vdash P$ then $\Gamma \vDash P$. It is *strongly complete* iff for every set Γ of closed formulas and every closed formula P, if $\Gamma \vDash P$ then $\Gamma \vdash P$.

(1.15) If a system of derivations is strongly sound then it is sound, and if it is strongly complete then it is complete.

Proof: Suppose a system of derivations is strongly sound. Suppose P is a theorem. Then $\emptyset \vdash P$. It follows by strong soundness that $\emptyset \vDash P$, and hence by theorem (1.7), $\vDash P$. The second half of the proof is analogous and is left as an exercise.

The following theorem provides a useful reformulation of strong soundness and strong completeness:

(1.16)   PC-derivations are strongly sound iff every satisfiable set of closed formulas is consistent, and PC-derivations are strongly complete iff every consistent set of closed formulas is satisfiable.

Proof: Suppose PC-derivations are strongly sound. Suppose Γ is inconsistent. Then for some Q, $\Gamma \vdash (Q \, \& \sim Q)$. As PC-derivations are strongly sound, $\Gamma \vDash (Q \, \& \sim Q)$. Thus every model of Γ is a model of $(Q \, \& \sim Q)$. But $(Q \, \& \sim Q)$ has no models, so Γ has no models, i.e., Γ is unsatisfiable.

The rest of the proof is analogous and is left as an exercise.

It is quite easy to establish that PC-derivations are strongly sound. We begin by noting that for each rule of inference for PC-derivations, the corresponding principle regarding implication also holds. For instance, corresponding to (**KE**) we have:

$$\text{If } \Gamma \vDash (P \, \& \, Q) \text{ then } \Gamma \vDash P \text{ and } \Gamma \vDash Q.$$

Let us say that a line $\langle \Gamma, P \rangle$ of a PC-derivation is *sound* just in case $\Gamma \vDash P$. We then prove by mathematical induction that for any n, the first $n+1$ lines of a PC-derivation are sound. For the basis, suppose $\langle \Gamma, P \rangle$ is the first line. The only rules that can be employed for introducing the first line are (**P**) and (**=I**). If $\langle \Gamma, P \rangle$ is introduced by (**P**) then $P \in \Gamma$, in which case $\Gamma \vDash P$. If instead $\langle \Gamma, P \rangle$ is introduced by (**=I**) then $\Gamma = \emptyset$ and P is $\ulcorner c = c \urcorner$. But then P is valid, so $\emptyset \vDash P$. So the first line of a derivation must be sound.

For the induction step, suppose the first $n+1$ lines of a derivation are sound, and prove that the $(n+2)$nd line is sound. This amounts to showing that the use of any rule of PC-derivations to add a line to a sequence of sound lines will result in the new line being sound. For instance, suppose we use (**KE**). Then $\langle \Gamma, (P \, \& \, Q) \rangle$ occurs among the first $n+1$ lines. By hypothesis, this line is sound, so $\Gamma \vDash (P \, \& \, Q)$. But then $\Gamma \vDash P$. So $\langle \Gamma, P \rangle$ is also sound. Similar reasoning establishes for each rule that its use will result in the addition of a sound line.

It follows by mathematical induction that every line of a PC-derivation is sound, and hence:

(1.17)   **Strong Soundness of PC-derivations**:   If $\Gamma \vdash P$ then $\Gamma \vDash P$.

As a corollary we have:

(1.18)   **Soundness of PC-derivations**:   If $\vdash P$ then $\vDash P$.

PC-derivations can be derivations of formulas from infinite sets. That is, we can have lines $\langle \Gamma, P \rangle$ in derivations where Γ is infinite. But such a derivation never makes use of more than finitely many members of Γ. In any PC-derivation, all rules except rule (**P**) require the premise set Γ to be either the same as the premise set of some previous line or the union of the premise sets of two previous lines. Only rule (**P**) introduces "new" premise sets. Suppose we start with a derivation σ and construct a new derivation σ^* from it in the following way. First, whenever we use rule (**P**) to introduce a line $\langle \Gamma, P \rangle$, we replace it with the simpler line $\langle \{P\}, P \rangle$. Then we change the other lines accordingly so that their premise sets are chosen in accordance with the rules of inference used on those lines. The result is that for each line $\langle \Gamma, P \rangle$ in σ the corresponding line in σ^* has the form $\langle \Gamma^*, P \rangle$ where Γ^* is a finite subset of Γ. It follows that whenever there is a derivation of a line $\langle \Gamma, P \rangle$, there is also a derivation of a line $\langle \Gamma^*, P \rangle$ where Γ^* is some finite subset of Γ. This has two consequences:

(1.19)   If $\Gamma \vdash P$ then there is some finite subset Γ^* of Γ such that $\Gamma^* \vdash P$.

(1.20)   If Γ is inconsistent then some finite subset of Γ is inconsistent.

PC-derivations are also strongly complete, but this is much harder to prove. The first completeness proof was given by Kurt Gödel in 1931, but most modern proofs follow a proof first constructed by Leon Henkin. The proof is constructed in accordance with theorem (1.16). That is, we prove that every consistent set of closed formulas has a model. The proof proceeds in the following manner. We start with a consistent set Γ of closed formulas. We then construct a list of all the closed formulas of the language. The list will be constructed in a certain way. We go through the formulas in the list in order, and for each formula we add it to the set consisting of Γ and whatever we have already added to Γ provided we can do so consistently. Let Ω be the resulting set of sentences. It is then shown that Ω "describes" a model in the sense that Ω is the set of all closed formulas true in some particular model. Thus Ω has a model, and as Γ ⊆ Ω, this is also a model of Γ. This is the bare bones of the argument. The actual construction of the ordering and the proof that Ω describes a model gets complicated. In order to make our proof work, we must make an assumption about how many formulas there are in the language. We have assumed that there are infinitely many, but there are different sizes of infinities. We will assume specifically that there are the same number of closed formulas as there are natural numbers. Such a set is said to be *denumerable*. Denumerable sets are the smallest infinite sets. The assumption that the set of closed formulas is denumerable has the consequence that the set of closed formulas can be put into a one-one correspondence with the set of natural numbers. Such a correspondence is an *enumeration* of the formulas. For each number n, we can then talk about the nth formula in the enumeration. In fact, the assumption that there are denumerably many closed formulas is not essential to the completeness proof. Basically the same proof can be carried out without that assumption, but it requires the use of transfinite induction rather than ordinary mathematical induction. That is something we have not discussed, so I will avoid it here.

In order to prove completeness, we first define:

Def: Γ is *maximal consistent* iff Γ is a consistent set of closed formulas and for every closed formula P, either $P \in Γ$ or $\ulcorner \sim P \urcorner \in Γ$.

Maximal consistent sets have the following simple properties:

(1.21)   If Γ is maximal consistent and Γ ⊢ P then $P \in Γ$.

Proof: Suppose Γ is maximal consistent and Γ ⊢ P.   Then if

⌜∼P⌝∈Γ, we would also have Γ ⊢ ∼P, so Γ would be inconsistent. Thus ⌜∼P⌝∉Γ, and hence by maximality, P∈Γ.

(1.22) If Γ is maximal consistent and P is a closed formula then ⌜∼P⌝∈Γ iff P∉Γ.

Proof: By maximality, either P∈Γ or ⌜∼P⌝∈Γ, and by consistency they cannot both be in Γ.

(1.23) If Γ is maximal consistent and P and Q are closed formulas then ⌜(P & Q)⌝∈Γ iff P∈Γ and Q∈Γ.

Proof: exercise

Next define:

Def: Γ is ω-*complete* iff Γ is a set of closed formulas and for every existential generalization ⌜(∃x)P⌝ in Γ, Γ also contains some instance $Sb(c/x)P$ of the generalization.

(1.24) If Γ is maximal consistent and ω-complete then ⌜(∃x)P⌝∈Γ iff for some constant c, $Sb(c/x)P∈Γ$.

The completeness theorem follows from two lemmas, the first of which is:

(1.25) If Γ is maximal consistent and ω-complete then Γ has a model.

Proof: Suppose Γ is maximal consistent and ω-complete. We construct a model as follows. For each individual constant c we let [c] be {d| d is a constant & ⌜c = d⌝∈Γ}. Let D = {[c]| c is a constant}. We define μ as follows:
   (1) if P is a sentence letter, μ(P) = 1 iff P∈Γ;
   (2) if c is a constant, μ(c) = [c];
   (3) if R is an n-place relation symbol (n > 0), μ(R)
        = {⟨[c_1],...,[c_n]⟩| ⌜Rc_1,...,c_n⌝∈Γ}.
Now we can prove by induction on the length of a formula that a closed formula P is a member of Γ iff it is true in ⟨D,μ⟩. Suppose this holds for all formulas shorter than P, and let us show that it holds for P. We have six cases to consider:

(a) Suppose P is a sentence letter. Then by construction, P is true in $\langle D,\mu \rangle$ iff $\mu(P) = 1$.

(b) Suppose $P = \ulcorner c = d \urcorner$. If $P \in \Gamma$ then by (1.21), for any constant b, $\ulcorner c = b \urcorner \in \Gamma$ iff $\ulcorner d = b \urcorner \in \Gamma$, and hence $[c] = [d]$. Hence $\mu(c) = \mu(d)$, so $\ulcorner c = d \urcorner$ is true in $\langle D,\mu \rangle$. Conversely, if $\ulcorner c = d \urcorner$ is true in $\langle D,\mu \rangle$ then $[c] = [d]$. $d \in [d]$, so $d \in [c]$, and hence $\ulcorner c = d \urcorner \in \Gamma$.

(c) Suppose $P = \ulcorner Rc_1...c_n \urcorner$. Then P is true in $\langle D,\mu \rangle$ iff $\langle \mu(c_1),...,\mu(c_n) \rangle \in \mu(R)$, iff $\langle [c_1],...,[c_n] \rangle \in \mu(R)$, iff $\ulcorner Rc_1...c_n \urcorner \in \Gamma$.

(d) Suppose $P = \ulcorner \sim Q \urcorner$. $\sim Q$ is true in $\langle D,\mu \rangle$ iff Q is not true in $\langle D,\mu \rangle$, which by the induction hypothesis holds iff $Q \notin \Gamma$, which by (1.22) holds iff $\ulcorner \sim Q \urcorner \in \Gamma$.

(e) Suppose $P = \ulcorner (Q \ \& \ R) \urcorner$. This is analogous to (d), using (1.23).

(f) Suppose $P = \ulcorner (\exists x)Q \urcorner$. Suppose $P \in \Gamma$. By ω-completeness, for some constant c, $Sb(c/x)Q \in \Gamma$. Then by the induction hypothesis, $Sb(c/x)Q$ is true in $\langle D,\mu \rangle$, so $(\exists x)Q$ is true in $\langle D,\mu \rangle$. Conversely, suppose $(\exists x)Q$ is true in $\langle D,\mu \rangle$. Then for some constant c, $[c]$ satisfies Q in $\langle D,\mu \rangle$. c designates $[c]$ in $\langle D,\mu \rangle$, so it follows that $Sb(c/x)Q$ is true in $\langle D,\mu \rangle$. Then by the induction hypothesis, $Sb(c/x)Q \in \Gamma$. Hence by (1.21), $\ulcorner (\exists x)Q \urcorner \in \Gamma$.

Our second major lemma is:

(1.26)   If Γ is a consistent set of closed formulas and there are infinitely many individual constants not occurring in Γ then there is a maximal consistent ω-complete set Ω such that $\Gamma \subseteq \Omega$.

Proof: Suppose Γ is a consistent set of closed formulas and there are infinitely many individual constants not occurring in Γ. Consider an enumeration of all closed formulas, i.e., a 1-1 mapping f from ω onto the set of closed formulas, and consider the resulting ordering of closed formulas. We want to rearrange this ordering in such a way that whenever an existential generalization $\ulcorner (\exists x)Q \urcorner$ occurs, the next formula in the ordering is an instance of it $Sb(c/x)Q$ where c is a constant not occurring in any of the formulas preceding it in the ordering or in any members of Γ. This can always be done. As there are infinitely many constants not occurring in members of Γ, and every formula occurs at some point in the ordering, at each point in the ordering there will remain infinitely many constants that have not yet occurred. We simply proceed through the ordering to the first instance $Sb(c/x)Q$ where c has not previously occurred, and move that instance up so that it immediately follows the existential generalization. Repeating this process indefinitely yields an enumeration with the desired property. For each n, let P_n be the nth formula in the enumeration. So if P_n is an existential generalization $\ulcorner(\exists x)Q\urcorner$ then P_{n+1} is an instance $Sb(c/x)Q$ where c is a constant not occurring in any of the previous P_i's or in any member of Γ.

Now we define the sets A_i inductively as follows:

$A_0 = \Gamma$
$A_{i+1} = A_i \cup \{P_i\}$ if this is consistent, and $A_{i+1} = A_i \cup \{\sim P_i\}$
      otherwise.
$\Omega = \bigcup \{A_i \mid i \in \omega\}$.

For each i, either $P_i \in A_{i+1}$ or $\ulcorner \sim P_i \urcorner \in A_{i+1}$, so Ω is maximal. We prove by induction that each A_i is consistent. By hypothesis, A_0 is consistent. Suppose A_i is consistent. If A_{i+1} were inconsistent, it would have to be $A_i \cup \{\sim P_i\}$ where $A_i \cup \{P_i\}$ is inconsistent. But then both $A_i \cup \{\sim P_i\}$ and $A_i \cup \{P_i\}$ are inconsistent, i.e., both imply contradictions. Then $A_i \vdash \sim \sim P_i$ and $A_i \vdash \sim P_i$, and hence A_i is inconsistent, which contradicts the induction hypothesis. Therefore, A_{i+1} is consistent. It follows from this that Ω is consistent, because if Ω were inconsistent then by (1.20) it would have a finite inconsistent subset $\{Q_1,...,Q_k\}$. Each of these would either be in Γ or in some A_i, and as the A_i's are cumulative, there would be an i such that $\{Q_1,...,Q_k\} \subseteq A_i$. Then A_i would be inconsistent, contrary to what we have proven. Therefore, Ω is maximal consistent.

To prove that Ω is ω-complete, suppose $\ulcorner(\exists x)Q\urcorner \in \Omega$. For some i, $\ulcorner(\exists x)Q\urcorner$ is P_i. As $P_i \in \Omega$, P_i must be consistent with A_i. P_{i+1} is $Sb(c/x)Q$ for some c not occurring in any members of A_i. If P_{i+1} were inconsistent with A_{i+1}, then for some R, $A_{i+1} \cup \{Sb(c/x)Q\} \vdash (R \& \sim R)$. But then by (EI), $A_{i+1} \cup \{(\exists x)Q\} \vdash (R \& \sim R)$. $A_{i+1} \cup \{(\exists x)Q\} = A_{i+1}$, so A_{i+1} would be inconsistent, which contradicts our previous result. Hence P_{i+1} must be consistent with A_{i+1}, and hence $P_{i+1} \in A_{i+2}$. Thus $\ulcorner Sb(c/x)Q\urcorner \in \Omega$, and hence Ω is ω-complete.

It follows from (1.25) and (1.26) that if Γ is consistent and there are infinitely many individual constants not occurring in members of Γ, then Γ has a model. On the other hand, if Γ is consistent but there fail to be infinitely many individual constants not occurring in members of Γ, we can just extend the language by adding infinitely many new constants. That does not alter the semantics. Γ, as a set of formulas of this enlarged language, has a model, and hence it has a model as a set of formulas of the original language. Therefore:

(1.27)   ***Strong Completeness Theorem for PC-Derivations***:   If Γ is any consistent set of closed formulas then Γ has a model.

Combining strong completeness and strong soundness we get:

(1.28)   If Γ is a set of closed formulas then Γ is consistent iff it is satisfiable.

A surprising consequence of (1.28) is the ***Compactness theorem*** for the predicate calculus:

(1.29)   A set of closed formulas is satisfiable iff every finite subset of it is satisfiable.

Proof: Obviously, if Γ is satisfiable then every subset of it (finite or not) is satisfiable. Conversely, suppose every finite subset of Γ is satisfiable. By (1.29), every finite subset of Γ is consistent, and then by (1.20), Γ is consistent. Then by (1.29), Γ is satisfiable.

1.4 *Definite Descriptions*
Following Bertrand Russell, we take the definite description $\iota x G x$ to be "defined contextually". This means that we do not give a definition of the expression itself, but rather of formulas containing it. In the simplest case, where F is a monadic relation symbol:

Def: $\ulcorner F(\iota x G x)\urcorner = \ulcorner (\exists x)[Fx\ \&\ (\forall y)(Gy \equiv y = x)]\urcorner$.

We cannot employ this same definition in general, however,

because if we let $\ulcorner\!\!\sim\!F(\iota xGx)\urcorner = \ulcorner(\exists x)[\sim\!Fx\ \&\ (\forall y)(Gy \equiv y = x)]\urcorner$, this has the result that $\sim\!F(\iota xGx)$ is not the negation of $F(\iota xGx)$. Instead, both would have "existential import", i.e., both would imply $\ulcorner(\exists x)(\forall y)(Gy \equiv y = x)\urcorner$. The latter says that there is such a thing as "the thing that is G". Let us express this as follows:

Def: $\ulcorner E!\iota xGx\urcorner = \ulcorner(\exists x)(\forall y)(Gy \equiv y = x)\urcorner$.

$\ulcorner E!\iota xGx\urcorner$ makes a contingent claim, so it should not be implied by both a formula and its negation (otherwise both would be false if the contingent claim were false). Formulas containing definite descriptions have two kinds of negations—*internal negations* and *external negations*. The external negation of $F(\iota xGx)$ is the ordinary negation, i.e.,

$$\sim\!(\exists x)[Fx\ \&\ (\forall y)(Gy \equiv y = x)].$$

The internal negation says instead that there is such a thing as the G, and it is not F:

$$(\exists x)[\sim\!Fx\ \&\ (\forall y)(Gy \equiv y = x)].$$

We symbolize the latter as:

Def: $\ulcorner[\sim\!Fx](\iota xGx)\urcorner = \ulcorner(\exists x)[\sim\!Fx\ \&\ (\forall y)(Gy \equiv y = x)]\urcorner$.

The difference between $\ulcorner F(\iota xGx)\urcorner$ and $\ulcorner[\sim\!Fx](\iota xGx)\urcorner$ is said to lie in the *scope* of the definite description. We define in general:

Def: If φ is an n-formula having free occurrences of the variables $x_1,...,x_n$ (listed in some fixed ordering), and $\theta_1,...,\theta_n$ are 1-formulas whose free variables are $x_1,...,x_n$ respectively, then $\ulcorner[\varphi](\iota x_1\theta_1,...,\iota x_n\theta_n)\urcorner = \ulcorner(\exists x_1)...(\exists x_n)\{\varphi\ \&\ (\forall x_1)(Sb(y/x_1)\theta_1 \equiv y = x_1)\ \&\ ...\ \&\ (\forall x_n)(Sb(y/x_n)\theta_n \equiv y = x_n)\}\urcorner$.

In $\ulcorner[\varphi](\iota x_1\theta_1,...,\iota x_n\theta_n)\urcorner$, $[\varphi]$ is the *scope* of the definite descriptions. It is important to pay attention to the scopes of definite descriptions. English sentences are typically ambiguous in this respect, and that has played a role in the generation of fallacious arguments that have actually been quite influential in the history of philosophy.

It is convenient to do away with the scope notation for atomic formulas:

Def: If R is a n-ary relation symbol then $\ulcorner R(\iota x_1\theta_1,...,\iota x_n\theta_n)\urcorner =$
$\ulcorner [Rx_1,...,x_n](\iota x\theta_1,...,\iota x\theta_n)\urcorner$.

Def: $\ulcorner \iota xP = \iota xQ\urcorner = \ulcorner [x = y](\iota xP,\iota yQ)\urcorner$.

There are some simple theorems about the effects of non-atomic scopes:

(1.30) $\ulcorner [\sim\varphi](\iota x_1\theta_1,...,\iota x_n\theta_n)\urcorner$ is equivalent to $\ulcorner E!\iota x_1\theta_1$ & ... & $E!\iota x_n\theta_n$ & $\ulcorner \sim[\varphi](\iota x_1\theta_1,...,\iota x_n\theta_n)\urcorner$.

(1.31)   If φ and ψ are n-formulas then $\ulcorner [(\varphi \, \& \, \psi)](\iota x_1\theta_1,...,\iota x_n\theta_n)\urcorner$ is equivalent to $\ulcorner [\varphi](\iota x_1\theta_1,...,\iota x_n\theta_n)$ & $[\psi](\iota x_1\theta_1,...,\iota x_n\theta_n)\urcorner$.

(1.32) $\ulcorner [(\exists y)\varphi](\iota x_1\theta_1,...,\iota x_n\theta_n)\urcorner$ is equivalent to
$\ulcorner (\exists y)[\varphi](\iota x_1\theta_1,...,\iota x_n\theta_n)\urcorner$.

By repeated application of (1.30)−(1.32), the scopes of the definite descriptions in a formula can be systematically driven inward until they become atomic. Thus we could, without loss of expressive power, have required that the scopes of definite descriptions always be atomic.

A further result can be proven on the basis of (1.30)−(1.32). The only effect of varying the scope is to alter the existential import, and that only occurs in the case of negations (in accordance with (1.30)). Thus if we know that the definite descriptions have denotations, the scopes should not make any difference to anything. More precisely,

(1.33) $\ulcorner E!\iota x_1\theta_1$ & ... & $E!\iota x_n\theta_n\urcorner$ implies
$\ulcorner [\varphi](\iota x_1\theta_1,...,\iota x_n\theta_n) \equiv Sb(\iota x_1\theta_1,...,\iota x_n\theta_n/x_1,...,x_n)\varphi\urcorner$.

In this equivalence, $\ulcorner Sb(\iota x_1\theta_1,...,\iota x_n\theta_n/x_1,...,x_n)\varphi\urcorner$ is a formula in which definite descriptions have only atomic scopes. This theorem is proven by induction on the length of φ, using (1.30)−(1.32). In many cases in which we use definite descriptions, we will know that the terms have denotations, so this theorem will allow us to ignore scopes.

1.5 First-Order Logic with Functions

In most concrete applications of the predicate calculus, we want to be able to symbolize propositions about functions. For instance, in axiomatizing arithmetic we will want to talk about addition, multiplication, and exponentiation. There are two ways of handling functions in the predicate calculus. The most straightforward is to extend the language, adding a new class of primitive symbols. We would call these *function symbols*, and we would add new formulas to the language to allow us to write things like $\ulcorner R(f(x),g(y))\urcorner$. Proceeding in that way is straightforward but tedious because it requires us to repeat all of our previous work on semantics and derivations and verify that it still works with the addition of function symbols.

There is another alternative available to us, and it will be followed here. We can get the effect of function symbols, without changing the language, by using definite descriptions. An n-place function $f(x_1,...,x_n)$ can be identified with an $(n+1)$-place relation $f(x_1,...,x_n,y)$, and then we can introduce function notation by letting $\ulcorner f(x_1,...,x_n)\urcorner$ be an abbreviation for $\ulcorner \iota y\, f(x_1,...,x_n,y)\urcorner$. If we know that our functions are defined for everything in our universe of discourse (i.e., their domains include all n-tuples of elements from our universe of discourse), then in light of theorem (1.33), we do not have to worry about scopes and can treat terms of the form $\ulcorner f(x_1,...,x_n)\urcorner$ just as if they were individual constants or variables.

Practice exercise: Treating $\ulcorner x + y\urcorner$ as a more perspicuous way of writing $\ulcorner +(x,y)\urcorner$, write the formula $\ulcorner (\forall x)(\forall y)\, x + y = y + x\urcorner$ in primitive notation (that is, without function symbols or definite descriptions).

2. First-Order Theories

2.1 Axiomatic Theories

One of the main uses of the predicate calculus is in axiomatizing various subject matters. The most common case is the axiomatization of mathematical theories, but we also find axiomatizations of physical theories, theories of measurement, economic theories, and so forth. In general, a *first-order theory* is any set of closed formulas closed under implication:

Def: T is a first-order theory iff T is a set of closed formulas and for any P, if T $\models P$ then $P \in$ T.

The *theorems* of a theory are its members. An *axiomatization* of T is simply a set of formulas in T that imply all the other theorems of T. Trivially, every theory is axiomatizable—we can let every theorem be an axiom. The more interesting case is that of finitely axiomatizable theories:

Def: A first-order theory T is *finitely axiomatizable* iff there is a finite subset A of T such that for every P in T, $A \models P$.

Def: A first-order theory T is *consistent* iff it is a consistent set of closed formulas.

Usually in constructing a theory, we have in mind a particular model, which we call *the intended model*. Such a theory is said to be an *interpreted first-order theory*. For example, in axiomatizing arithmetic the domain of the intended model is ω and we use a language in which the only relation symbols are symbols expressing addition, multiplication, and exponentiation. In such a case, every closed formula has a unique truth value in the intended model, and a satisfactory axiomatization should make every true formula a theorem. We can define notions of soundness and completeness relative to the intended model:

Def: An interpreted first-order theory T is *sound* iff all of its theorems are true in the intended model.

Def: An interpreted first-order theory T is *semantically complete* iff all formulas true in the intended model are theorems.

For every formula, either it or its negation is true in the intended model, so we can also generate a more syntactical notion of completeness:

Def: An interpreted first-order theory **T** is *(simply) complete* iff for every closed formula P, either $P \in$ T or $\ulcorner \sim P \urcorner \in$ T.

There are some simple relationships between these different notions:

(2.1)   If **T** is an interpreted first-order theory then:
  (a)   if **T** is sound, then **T** is complete iff **T** is semantically complete;
  (b)   if **T** is unsound, then if **T** is consistent, it is semantically incomplete;
  (c)   if **T** is semantically complete, then **T** is sound iff **T** is consistent.

Proof of (a): Suppose **T** is sound. Every closed formula is either true or false in the intended model, so if **T** is complete then it is semantically complete. Conversely, suppose **T** is semantically complete but not complete. Then there is some true formula P that is not a theorem. But then $\sim P$ is a theorem, which is impossible as **T** is sound.

   (b) and (c) are left as exercises.

A number of important examples of complete theories are known. For example, Tarski has shown that there is a complete finite axiomatization of the theory of the arithmetic of the real numbers. Early progress in constructing axiomatizations led mathematicians to think that all of mathematics should be axiomatizable, and to suggest that mathematical truth might just consist of being the logical consequences of conventionally adopted axioms. In this context, Gödel's theorem was earthshaking. What Gödel showed was that no powerful mathematical theories are axiomatizable in any interesting way. That is our next topic.

2.2 Semantic Closure

   Theories that are ostensibly about one topic can often be reinterpreted in such a way that they can be regarded as encoding information about a totally different topic. In particular, they may be "semantically closed" in a way that enables them to encode information about themselves. Consider a first-order theory **T** with infinitely many individual constants. The individual constants will, in the intended interpretation, denote numbers or sets or something like that, but we can reinterpret them to represent formulas of the language of the theory. Define:

Def: η is a *Gödel function for T* iff η maps the set of formulas and finite sequences of formulas 1-1 into the set of individual constants. If the constants are numerals (i.e., they designate natural numbers), η is said to be a *Gödel numbering*.

We can think of $\eta(P)$ as playing the role of a "name" for the formula *P* in the nonstandard interpretation we are constructing. To illustrate this, consider a formalization of first-order number theory (the arithmetic of the natural numbers) in which we express addition, multiplication, and exponentiation in the normal ways, and we have a constant for each number (its numeral). A Gödel numbering can be constructed using what is called "the prime factorization theorem". Prime numbers are numbers divisible only by themselves and 1. The primes are 1,2,3,5,7,11,13,17,19,23,... . There are infinitely many prime numbers. The prime factorization theorem tells us that every natural number can be represented in just one way as a product of powers of primes. For instance,

$$11643588 = 2^2 \cdot 3^7 \cdot 11^3$$

To construct a Gödel numbering for first-order number theory, we begin by enumerating the primitive symbols of the language in the following way:

~	1
&	2
∃	3
(	4
)	5
+	6
•	7
exp	8
=	9
0	10
x	11

1	12
y	13

$\cdot$

$\cdot$

$\cdot$

We complete this list with an enumeration of the rest of the variables and constants (the latter are numerals) ordered in such a way that they alternate (to make a single enumeration possible). Each formula is a finite sequence of primitive symbols, so we construct its Gödel number as the product of powers of primes where the first term is the second prime (that is, 2) raised to the power of the number corresponding to that primitive symbol, the second term is the next prime raised to the power of the number corresponding to that primitive symbol, and so on. For instance, the Gödel number of $\ulcorner(\exists x)(\exists y)(x+y = x \cdot y)\urcorner$ is

$$2^4 \cdot 3^3 \cdot 5^{11} \cdot 7^5 \cdot 11^4 \cdot 13^3 \cdot 17^{13} \cdot 19^5 \cdot 23^4 \cdot 29^{11} \cdot 31^6 \cdot 37^{13} \cdot 41^9 \cdot 43^7 \cdot 47^{13} \cdot 53^5$$

In this way we get a Gödel number for each formula. Gödel numbers for finite sequences of formulas are constructed analogously. The Gödel number for the sequence $\langle P_1,...,P_n \rangle$ is taken to be:

$$p_1{}^{\eta(P_1)} \cdot ... \cdot p_n{}^{\eta(P_n)}$$

where for each i, p_i is the $(i+1)$th prime number. We can then regard the numeral (individual constant) denoting this number as a name of the formula.

Given a Gödel numbering, we can regard formulas of the object language as "expressing" formulas of the metalanguage in the following sense:

Def: If **T** is an interpreted theory, η is a Gödel function, $\Sigma(P_1,...,P_n)$ is a metalinguistic formula whose free metalinguistic variables are $P_1,...,P_n$, and $\psi(x_1,...,x_n)$ is an n-formula of **T**, ψ *expresses* Σ in **T** iff for all formulas $P_1,...,P_n$, $\Sigma(P_1,...,P_n)$ is true iff $\psi(\eta(P_1),...,\eta(P_n))$ is true in the intended model.

For instance, in the Gödel numbering just constructed, the Gödel numbers of variables are all the odd numbers greater than 9, so the metalinguistic formula "α is a variable" is expressed by the object language formula

$$x > 9 \ \& \ \sim(\exists y) \ x = 2 \cdot y.$$

In a similar way, in any reasonably rich object language (for instance, number theory or set theory), given any a finite set of axioms we will be able to construct object language formulas expressing "α is an axiom" and "α is a derivation of β from the axioms".

We have defined what it is for an object language formula to express a metalinguistic formula. We can also talk about an object language *function* expressing a metalinguistic function:

Def: If $F(P_1,...,P_n)$ is a metalinguistic function and $f(x_1,...,x_n)$ is an object language function, f expresses F iff the object language formula $\ulcorner f(x_1,...,x_n) = y \urcorner$ expresses the metalinguistic formula "$F(P_1,...,P_n) = Q$".

There is a metalinguistic function, called the *diagonal function*, that plays a crucial role in Gödel's theorem and theorems about semantic closure:

Def: Δ is a one-place metalinguistic function defined by stipulating that for any 1-formula $\psi(x)$, $\Delta(\psi(x)) = \psi(\eta(\psi(x)))$.[1]

Note that $\psi(\eta(\psi(x)))$ can be interpreted as saying that the formula $\psi(x)$ satisfies itself. In any reasonably expressive object language, for instance, number theory, it will be simple to construct a formula expressing the diagonal function.

The following *Semantical Diagonalization Theorem* is the crucial lemma for results on semantic closure:

---

[1] A less perspicuous but technically more accurate way of writing this definition would be as follows: Δ is a one-place metalinguistic function defined by stipulating that for any 1-formula ψ, if x is the single free variable of ψ then $\Delta(\psi) = Sb(\eta(\psi)/x)\psi$.

(2.2)   If **T** is an interpreted first-order theory for which there is a Gödel function η, and Δ is expressible in **T**, then given any 1-formula $\psi(x)$ there is a closed formula θ such that $\ulcorner\theta \equiv \psi(\eta(\theta))\urcorner$ is true in the intended model.

Proof: Suppose $\delta(x)$ expresses Δ. Let $\theta = \psi(\delta(\eta(\psi(\delta(x)))))$. $\Delta(\psi(\delta(x))) = \psi(\delta(\eta(\psi(\delta(x)))))$, so as δ expresses Δ, $\ulcorner\delta(\eta(\psi(\delta(x)))) = \eta(\psi(\delta(\eta(\psi(\delta(x))))))\urcorner$ is true in the intended model. That is, $\ulcorner\delta(\eta(\psi(\delta(x)))) = \eta(\theta)\urcorner$ is true in the intended model. Trivially, $\ulcorner\psi(\delta(\eta(\psi(\delta(x))))) \equiv \psi(\delta(\eta(\psi(\delta(x)))))\urcorner$ is true in the intended model, so by the substitutivity of identity, substituting $\eta(\theta)$ for $\ulcorner\delta(\eta(\psi(\delta(x))))\urcorner$ in this biconditional, we obtain that $\ulcorner\psi(\delta(\eta(\psi(\delta(x))))) \equiv \psi(\eta(\theta))\urcorner$ is true in the intended model. But this is just $\ulcorner\theta \equiv \psi(\eta(\theta))\urcorner$.

We have the following simple theorem, more or less due to Tarski, which is of very profound significance:

(2.3)   If **T** is an interpreted first-order theory for which there is a Gödel function η, and Δ is expressible in **T**, then *truth* (i.e., the metalinguistic formula "α is true in the intended model") is not expressible in **T**.

Proof: The proof is modeled on the liar paradox. If truth were expressible in **T**, we could construct a formula that says of itself that it is not true. That formula would then be both true and not true, which is impossible. Making this precise, suppose **T** is an interpreted first-order theory for which there is a Gödel function η, and Δ is expressible in **T**. Suppose that there is an object language formula $T(x)$ that expresses the metalinguistic formula "α is true in the intended model". By the semantical diagonalization theorem, there is a formula θ such that $\ulcorner\theta \equiv \sim T(\eta(\theta))\urcorner$ is true in the intended model. Either θ or $\sim\theta$ is true in the intended model. Suppose θ is true. As $T(x)$ expresses truth, it follows that $T(\eta(\theta))$ is also true in the intended model. But that is impossible because $\ulcorner\theta \equiv \sim T(\eta(\theta))\urcorner$ is true in the intended model. Thus it must instead be $\sim\theta$ that is true in the intended model. Then θ is not true, so $T(\eta(\theta))$ is not true either. In other words, θ is false and $\sim T(\eta(\theta))$ is true. But this is again impossible because $\ulcorner\theta \equiv \sim T(\eta(\theta))\urcorner$ is true in the intended model. Thus we have a contradiction. So truth cannot be expressible in T.

From (2.3) we immediately obtain a very simple "semantical analogue" of Gödel's theorem:

(2.4)   If T is an interpreted sound first-order theory for which there is a Gödel function η, and Δ is expressible in T, and "α is a theorem of T" is expressible in T, then T is incomplete.

Proof: Suppose T is an interpreted sound first-order theory for which there is a Gödel function η, and Δ is expressible in T, and "α is a theorem of T" is expressible in T. If T were complete, a formula would satisfy "α is a theorem of T" iff it satisfied "α is true in the intended model". Thus an object language formula expressing "α is a theorem of T" would also express "α is true in the intended model". By (2.3), the latter is impossible, so T is not complete.

Suppose that T can be axiomatized by some set of axioms we know to be true. Then the proof of (2.4) is a proof of the truth of the Gödel formula θ (because θ is true iff it is not a theorem of T). Consequently, θ is provable without being derivable from the axioms of T. Hence this theorem is often regarded as telling us that provability outstrips derivability from any particular set of true axioms. This is a puzzling result.

(2.4) is not quite Gödel's theorem, for reasons I will explain in the next section, but it contains most of the philosophical meat of Gödel's theorem. As I indicated above, if T is any reasonably expressive theory, Δ will be expressible in it. This is true, for example, if T is first-order number theory, or if T is some theory like set theory within which first-order number theory can be constructed. If T has a finite set of axioms, then it will be quite mechanical to construct a formula expressing the metalinguistic formula "α is an axiom". Even if T has an infinite set of axioms (e.g., it might have axiom schemas), this will often remain true. And if "α is an axiom" is expressible, it is not at all difficult to construct a formula expressing "α is a derivation of β from the axioms". Suppose $Pr(x,y)$ is such a formula. Then "α is a theorem of T" is expressed by $\ulcorner(\exists x)Pr(x,y)\urcorner$. Thus, *no reasonably expressive sound first-order theory with a "well behaved" set of axioms can be complete.*

To illustrate this result, consider the first-order theory **S** known as *Peano arithmetic*. It has the following axioms:

$(\forall x)(\exists y)(\forall z)(Sxz \equiv z = y)$ (i.e., S is a function)
$(\forall x)(\forall y)(S(x) = S(y) \supset x = y)$
$(\forall x)S(x) \neq 0$
For any 1-formula $\psi(x)$, the following is an axiom:
    $[\psi(0) \;\&\; (\forall x)(\psi(x) \supset \psi(S(x)))] \supset (\forall x)\psi(x)$.
$(\forall x)x+0 = x$
$(\forall x)(\forall y)x+S(y) = S(x+y)$
$(\forall x)x \cdot 0 = 0$
$(\forall x)(\forall y)x \cdot S(y) = x \cdot y + x$
$(\forall x)x^0 = 1$
$(\forall x)(\forall y)x^{S(y)} = x^y \cdot x$.

The fourth item on this list is the *axiom scheme of induction*. It is an axiom scheme rather than a single axiom because it yields a separate axiom for each choice of ψ. The axioms of **S** appear to be just Peano's axioms together with the inductive definitions of addition, multiplication, and exponentiation. We know that the latter axioms completely characterize ω, so it seems surprising that **S** is incomplete. The explanation for why it is not has to do with the axiom scheme of induction. That does not fully express the induction principle. The easiest way to see this is to note that the axiom scheme only generates an instance for each property expressed by a 1-formula of the language of first-order number theory, but it can be proven that "most" properties of the natural numbers cannot be so expressed. More accurately, the set of all properties of the natural numbers is of a higher order of infinity than the set of 1-formulas. To fully express the principle of mathematical induction, we must use *second-order logic*, wherein we can quantify over properties as well as over numbers. We can then replace the axiom scheme by the single second-order axiom:

$$(\forall F)\{[F(0) \;\&\; (\forall x)(F(x) \supset F(S(x)))] \supset (\forall x)F(x)\}.$$

It can be shown that the resulting set of second-order axioms is complete. In fact, the proof of categoricity that we gave in set theory can be turned into a proof of completeness for the second-order axioms.

Practice exercise: Gödel's theorem leads to a distinction between "absolute provability" and "formal derivability from a set of axioms". Assume that anything that is provable absolutely is true. Given some interpreted theory **T**, suppose there is a number-theoretical predicate p of **T** that expresses absolute provability, i.e., which is such that for any closed formula P of **T**, P is provable absolutely iff $p(\eta(P))$ is true in the intended model of **T**. By the diagonalization theorem, there is a closed formula Q such that $\ulcorner Q \equiv \sim p(\eta(Q)) \urcorner$ is provable absolutely. Show that (1) Q is not provable absolutely, and (2) Q is true.

2.3 Gödel's Theorem

Theorem (2.4) was described as a "semantical analogue" of Gödel's theorem. Theorem (2.4) applies to interpreted theories and makes essential appeal to truth in the intended model. Gödel's theorem itself is entirely nonsemantical. Most of the philosophical meat of Gödel's theorem can be gotten out of (2.4), but there is some philosophical reason for preferring a nonsemantical theorem. This is that Gödel's theorem is used to throw light on the concept of mathematical truth itself. For this purpose we might be skeptical of "mathematical realism" according to which mathematical truth is understood literally in terms of a domain of mathematical objects. A natural and once popular alternative was to try to analyze mathematical truth in terms of provability from a purely conventional set of axioms. Such views of mathematical truth might undermine some of the semantical moves used in proving theorem (2.4). Gödel's theorem, by contrast, is not subject to such objections and is generally regarded as establishing that such a conventional view of mathematical truth is untenable. In fact, Gödel's theorem constitutes one of the principal tools used by some to defend mathematical realism.

Gödel's theorem replaces the use of "express" by the use of "represent":

Def: If $\Sigma(P_1,...,P_n)$ is a metalinguistic formula whose free metalinguistic variables are $P_1,...,P_n$, and $\psi(x_1,...,x_n)$ is an n-formula of **T**, ψ *represents* Σ in **T** iff for all formulas $P_1,...,P_n$:

(1)   if $\Sigma(P_1,...,P_n)$ is true then $\ulcorner\psi(\eta(P_1),...,\eta(P_n))\urcorner$ is a theorem of **T**; and

(2)   if $\Sigma(P_1,...,P_n)$ is false then $\ulcorner\sim\psi(\eta(P_1),...,\eta(P_n))\urcorner$ is a theorem of **T**.

Def: If $\Sigma(P_1,...,P_n)$ is a metalinguistic formula whose free metalinguistic variables are $P_1,...,P_n$, and $\psi(x_1,...,x_n)$ is an *n*-formula of **T**, ψ *weakly represents* Σ in **T** iff for all formulas $P_1,...,P_n$, if $\Sigma(P_1,...,P_n)$ is true then $\ulcorner\psi(\eta(P_1),...,\eta(P_n))\urcorner$ is a theorem of **T**.

Def: If $F(P_1,...,P_n)$ is a metalinguistic function and $f(x_1,...,x_n)$ is an object language function, *f* *represents* (or *weakly represents*) *F* iff the object language formula $\ulcorner f(x_1,...,x_n) = y\urcorner$ represents (or weakly represents) the metalinguistic formula "$F(P_1,...,P_n) = Q$".

In almost precisely the same way we proved the semantical diagonalization theorem (2.2), we prove *Tarski's Diagonalization Theorem*:

(2.5)   If Δ is weakly representable in **T**, then given any 1-formula $\psi(x)$ there is a closed formula θ such that $\ulcorner\theta \equiv \psi(\eta(\theta))\urcorner$ is a theorem of **T**.

Proof: exercise

Gödel's First Incompleteness Theorem is now the following:

(2.6)   If **T** is a first-order theory containing **S**, **T** is consistent, Δ is weakly representable, and "α is a proof of β" is representable, then **T** is incomplete.

Proof: Suppose **T** is a first-order theory containing **S**, **T** is consistent, Δ is weakly representable, and $Pr(x,y)$ represents "α is a proof of β". By the diagonalization theorem, we can choose a θ such that

$$\theta = (\forall x)(Pr(x,\eta(\theta)) \supset (\exists y)[y < x \ \& \ Pr(y,\eta(\sim\theta))])$$

is a theorem of **T**. Intuitively, θ "says of itself" that if there is a proof of it then there is a proof with a smaller Gödel number of $\sim\theta$. Now we prove that neither θ nor $\sim\theta$ is a theorem of **T**. Suppose θ is a theorem. Then for some sequence σ, σ is a proof of θ. Consequently, $Pr(\eta(\sigma),\eta(\theta))$ is also a theorem of **T**. As θ is a theorem, so is

$$(\forall x)\big(Pr(x,\eta(\theta)) \supset (\exists y)[y < x \ \& \ Pr(y,\eta(\sim\theta))]\big),$$

so

$$(\exists y)[y < \eta(\sigma) \ \& \ Pr(y,\eta(\sim\theta))]$$

is a theorem of **T**. For each numeral k, if $0,...,m$ are the preceding numerals, then the following is a theorem scheme of **S** and hence of **T**:

$$(\exists y)[y < k \ \& \ F(y)] \supset [F(0) \vee ... \vee F(m)].$$

Consequently, the following is a theorem of **T**:

$$Pr(0,\eta(\sim\theta)) \vee ... \vee Pr(m,\eta(\sim\theta))$$

where $0,...,m$ are the numerals preceding $\eta(\sigma)$. As $Pr(x,y)$ represents "α is a proof of β", if a numeral k is not the Gödel numeral for a proof of $\sim\theta$, then $\ulcorner\sim Pr(k,\eta(\sim\theta))\urcorner$ is a theorem of **T**. Consequently, if none of $0,...,m$ is a Gödel numeral for a proof of $\sim\theta$ then

$$\sim Pr(0,\eta(\sim\theta)) \ \& \ ... \ \& \ \sim Pr(m,\eta(\sim\theta))$$

is a theorem of **T**. But then **T** would be inconsistent, contrary to hypothesis. Thus one of $0,...,m$ must be the Gödel numeral for a proof of $\sim\theta$, and hence $\sim\theta$ is a theorem of **T**. But that is again impossible because we assumed that θ is a theorem of **T** and **T** is consistent. Therefore, θ is not a theorem of **T**.

Suppose $\sim\theta$ is a theorem of **T**. Then for some σ, σ is a proof of $\sim\theta$. Then $\ulcorner Pr(\eta(\sigma),\eta(\sim\theta))\urcorner$ is a theorem of **T**. As **T** is consistent, θ is not a theorem of **T**, so there is no proof of θ. Let

0,...,*m* be the numerals preceding $\eta(\sigma)$. As none of these is the Gödel numeral for a proof of θ,

$$\sim Pr(0,\eta(\theta)) \;\&\; ... \;\&\; \sim Pr(m,\eta(\theta)) \;\&\; \sim Pr(\eta(\sigma),\eta(\theta))$$

is a theorem of **T**. The latter implies in **S**, and hence in **T**,

$$(\forall x)[x \leq \eta(\sigma) \supset \sim Pr(x,\eta(\theta))].$$

This in turn implies

$$(\forall x)[Pr(x,\eta(\theta)) \supset \eta(\sigma) < x],$$

so this is a theorem of **T**. $\ulcorner Pr(\eta(\sigma),\eta(\sim\theta))\urcorner$ is also a theorem of **T**, so

$$(\forall x)[Pr(x,\eta(\theta)) \supset [\eta(\sigma) < x \;\&\; Pr(\eta(\sigma),\eta(\sim\theta))]]$$

is a theorem of **T**. This implies the following theorem of **T**:

$$(\forall x)[Pr(x,\eta(\theta)) \supset (\exists y)[y < x \;\&\; Pr(y,\eta(\sim\theta))]].$$

But θ was chosen so that it is equivalent in **T** to the latter, so θ is a theorem of **T**. Thus again, **T** is inconsistent. Consequently, $\sim\theta$ cannot be a theorem of **T**.

As neither θ nor $\sim\theta$ is a theorem of **T**, **T** is incomplete.

Although (2.6) is officially called "Gödel's theorem", this is not the form of the theorem proven by Gödel himself. This version of Gödel's theorem has profited from improvements by a number of mathematicians and logicians, the most notable being Rosser and Tarski.

The "crisis in set theory" engendered by the discovery of the set-theoretic antinomies led mathematicians and logicians to look for axiomatizations of set theory that could be proven consistent. Gödel's second incompleteness theorem is directed at that. It shows that if a theory **T** is strong enough to enable us to prove its own consistency within it, then **T** is actually inconsistent. Any convincing proof of consistency for an axiomatic set theory strong enough to found mathematics would have to be such that it could be carried out within that set theory itself, so it would then follow that the set theory is inconsistent. Consequently, the hope that some strong axiomatic set theory could be constructed that was demonstrably consistent has proven vain.

Consider a theory **T** strong enough for Δ to be weakly representable in it and "α is a proof of β" to be representable in it. Let $Pr(x,y)$ represent the latter, and define $\ulcorner Thm(x) \urcorner$ to be $\ulcorner (\exists y)Pr(y,x) \urcorner$. Then $\ulcorner Thm(x) \urcorner$ weakly represents "α is a theorem of **T**". We use the diagonalization theorem to construct the "Gödel formula" G:

Def: G is the formula constructed in accordance with the diagonalization theorem so that $\ulcorner G \equiv \sim Thm(\eta(G)) \urcorner$ is a theorem of **T**.

Def: $Con = \ulcorner \sim[Thm(\eta(G) \ \& \ Thm(\eta(\sim G)))] \urcorner$.

Con is a formula that can be regarded as saying that **T** is consistent. We prove two lemmas:

(2.7)   If **T** is consistent and Δ and theoremhood are weakly representable, then G is not a theorem of **T**.

Proof: Suppose G is a theorem of **T**. Then $\ulcorner Thm(\eta(G)) \urcorner$ is a theorem of **T**, so $\ulcorner \sim G \urcorner$ is a theorem of **T**. But that contradicts the assumption that **T** is consistent.

(2.8)   If Δ and theoremhood are weakly representable in **T** and for any closed formulas P and Q:
    (a) $\ulcorner Thm(\eta(P \equiv Q)) \supset [Thm(\eta(P)) \equiv Thm(\eta(Q))] \urcorner$ is a theorem of **T**; and
    (b) $\ulcorner Thm(\eta(P)) \supset Thm(\eta(Thm(\eta(P)))) \urcorner$ is a theorem of **T**;
    then $\ulcorner Thm(\eta(G)) \supset Thm(\eta(\sim G)) \urcorner$ is a theorem of **T**.

Proof: By (b),

$$Thm(\eta(G)) \supset Thm(\eta(Thm(\eta(G))))$$

is a theorem of **T**. $\ulcorner \sim G \equiv Thm(\eta(G)) \urcorner$ is a theorem of **T**, so

$$Thm(\eta(\sim G \equiv Thm(\eta(G))))$$

is a theorem of **T**. Then by (a)

$$Thm(\eta(\sim G)) \equiv Thm(\eta(Thm(\eta(G))))$$

is a theorem of **T**. So $\ulcorner Thm(\eta(G)) \supset Thm(\eta(\sim G))\urcorner$ is a theorem of **T**.

Part of the significance of (a) and (b) in (2.8) is that $\ulcorner Thm(\eta(P \equiv Q)) \supset [Thm(\eta(P)) \equiv Thm(\eta(Q))]\urcorner$ and $\ulcorner Thm(\eta(P)) \supset Thm(\eta(Thm(\eta(P))))\urcorner$ are both true, and so ought to be theorems in any reasonably strong theory. They are, for example, theorems of **S**. *Gödel's Second Incompleteness Theorem* is now:

(2.9) If Δ and theoremhood are weakly representable in **T** and for any closed formulas P and Q:

    (a) $\ulcorner Thm(\eta(P \equiv Q)) \supset [Thm(\eta(P)) \equiv Thm(\eta(Q))]\urcorner$ is a theorem of **T**; and

    (b) $\ulcorner Thm(\eta(P)) \supset Thm(\eta(Thm(\eta(P))))\urcorner$ is a theorem of **T**; and

    (c) *Con* is a theorem of **T**;

    then **T** is inconsistent.

Proof: Suppose (a), (b), and (c) hold. *Con* is equivalent to $\ulcorner Thm(\eta(G)) \supset \sim Thm(\eta(\sim G))\urcorner$, so this is a theorem of **T**. By virtue of this and (2.8),

$$Thm(\eta(G)) \supset [Thm(\eta(\sim G)) \ \& \ \sim Thm(\eta(\sim G))]$$

is a theorem of **T**, so $\ulcorner \sim Thm(\eta(G))\urcorner$ is a theorem of **T**. But G is equivalent to the latter, so G is a theorem of **T**. Then by (2.7), **T** is inconsistent.

Our theorems all have hypotheses to the effect that various metalinguistic formulas and functions are representable or weakly representable in **T**. We might wonder how generally this condition is going to be satisfied. It turns out that it is satisfied by any reasonable axiomatization that contains even a rather weak version of first-order number theory. As was pointed out above, first-order theories need not have finite axiomatizations. For example, S does not. But the axioms of an axiomatic theory ought to at least be well-behaved in the very general sense that we can tell in a mechanical way whether any given formula is an axiom. A set is said to be *decidable* iff there is a mechanical procedure (an *algorithm*) for determining whether something is a member of it. So the requirement on reasonable axiomatic theories is that the set of axioms should at least be decidable.

The notion of a decidable set has been investigated at length in modern logic. It is connected with the notion of a *computable function*. A computable function is one for which there is a mechanical procedure for computing its value in any case. Given a set X, the *characteristic function* of X is defined as follows:

$$f(x) = 1 \text{ if } x \in X;$$
$$f(x) = 0 \text{ if } x \notin X.$$

Obviously, X is decidable iff its characteristic function is computable. Earlier in this century, several analyses were proposed for the notion of a computable function of natural numbers. These included the notion of a recursive function, a Post computable function, and a Turing computable function. Very roughly, a Turing computable function is one that could be computed by a computer with an unlimited memory. It was subsequently shown that these are all equivalent. The thesis that they are exactly the computable functions of natural numbers is:

Church's Thesis: A function from natural numbers to natural numbers is computable iff it is recursive.

Today, Church's thesis is accepted almost universally. Note that it is not the kind of thesis that can be proven mathematically, because the notion of a computable function does not have a mathematical characterization. Instead, this is a kind of epistemological thesis, and the evidence for it is essentially inductive.

A set of natural numbers is recursive iff its characteristic function is recursive. Church's Thesis implies:

A set of natural numbers is decidable iff it is recursive.

The *Gödel number* of a formula is the natural number denoted by its Gödel numeral. A set of formulas is said to be recursive iff the corresponding set of Gödel numbers is recursive. If the function assigning Gödel numbers is computable, then the set of formulas is decidable iff the corresponding set of Gödel numbers is decidable, and hence Church's Thesis also implies:

A set of formulas is decidable iff it is recursive.

Any normal assignment of Gödel numbers is computable. For example, that constructed above is obviously computable. (Notice that this does not mean that it is recursive. It is not a function from natural numbers to natural numbers, so it cannot be recursive.)

Recursive functions are functions defined on the natural numbers. We can also define the concept of a *recursive metalinguistic function* as follows. Where F is a metalinguistic function of expressions, we can construct a corresponding number theoretic function f by stipulating that $f(n_1,...,n_m) = k$ iff $n_1,...,n_m,k$ are the Gödel numbers of some expressions $E_1,...,E_m,E_k$ and $F(E_1,...,E_m) = E_k$. Then we say that F is a recursive metalinguistic function iff f is a recursive number theoretic function. If the Gödel numbering is computable, then F is computable iff f is computable, because either could be computed by computing the other. Thus it follows from Church's thesis that:

A metalinguistic function is computable iff it is recursive.

We defined representability for metalinguistic formulas and metalinguistic functions. It is convenient to extend this to *sets* of formulas, saying that a 1-formula $\psi(x)$ represents a set A iff there is a metalinguistic formula $\Sigma(X)$ such that $\psi(x)$ represents $\Sigma(X)$ and A is the set of all expressions X such that $\Sigma(X)$ holds. Thus, for instance, we can talk indifferently about "α is an axiom" being representable or about the *set* of axioms being representable.

In light of these results, the set of axioms of an axiomatic theory is decidable iff the set of axioms is recursive. Now consider the very weak axiomatic number theory known as *Robinson's Arithmetic*, **RR**. It has the following finite set of axioms:

(1) $(\forall x)(\forall y)[S(x) = S(y) \supset x = y]$
(2) $(\forall x) \; 0 \neq S(x)$
(3) $(\forall x)[x \neq 0 \supset (\exists y)x = S(y)]$
(4) $(\forall x) \; x+0 = x$
(5) $(\forall x)(\forall y) \; x+S(y) = S(x+y)$
(6) $(\forall x) \; x \cdot 0 = 0$
(7) $(\forall x)(\forall y) \; x \cdot S(y) = x \cdot y + x$
(8) $(\forall x)(\forall y)(\forall z)(\forall v)(\forall u)(\forall w)[(y = x \cdot z + w \; \& \; w < x \; \&$
       $y = x \cdot v + u \; \& \; u < x) \supset w = u]$ (where $\ulcorner u < v \urcorner$ is
       $\ulcorner (\exists z)(z \neq 0 \; \& \; z+u = v) \urcorner$).

The following theorem can then be proven:

(2.10)   If **RR** is contained in **T** then: (1) if f is a recursive
         metalinguistic function then f is representable in **T**; and
         (2) all recursive sets of formulas are representable in **T**.

It is obvious by Church's thesis that Δ is recursive, so it follows
that if **RR** is contained in **T** then Δ is representable and hence
weakly representable. We thus obtain the following generalized
version of Gödel's first incompleteness theorem:

(2.11)   If **T** is a consistent first-order theory containing **RR**, and
         T has a recursive set of axioms, then **T** is incomplete.

We can obtain a generalized version of Gödel's second incompleteness theorem by noting the following theorem, which will not
be proven here:

(2.12)   If **T** has a recursive set of axioms and **T** contains **S** then
         for any closed formulas P and Q:
         (a) $\ulcorner Thm(\eta(P \equiv Q)) \supset [Thm(\eta(P)) \equiv Thm(\eta(Q))] \urcorner$ is a
               theorem of **T**; and
         (b) $\ulcorner Thm(\eta(P)) \supset Thm(\eta(Thm(\eta(P)))) \urcorner$ is a theorem of
               T.

Consequently, from (2.9) we obtain:

(2.13)   If **T** has a recursive set of axioms, **T** contains **S**, and *Con*
         is a theorem of **T**, then **T** is inconsistent.

A *decidable theory* is one for which there is a mechanical procedure for determining whether something is a theorem. Such a mechanical procedure is called a *decision procedure*. A decidable theory is just one whose set of theorems is decidable. One of the early hopes of mathematical logic was that a decision procedure could be found for all of mathematics or at least for large parts of mathematics. It follows from Gödel's theorem that that cannot be done. We first prove the following simple lemma:

(2.14)   If **T** is a theory in which Δ is weakly representable and theoremhood is representable, then **T** is inconsistent.

Proof: Suppose $Thm(x)$ represents theoremhood, and choose G as before such that $\ulcorner G \equiv {\sim}Thm(\eta(G))\urcorner$ is a theorem of **T**. Suppose G is not a theorem of **T**. Then $\ulcorner {\sim}Thm(\eta(G))\urcorner$ is a theorem of **T**, so G is a theorem of **T**. Therefore, G is a theorem of **T**. But then $\ulcorner Thm(\eta(G))\urcorner$ is a theorem of **T**, and hence $\ulcorner {\sim}G\urcorner$ is a theorem of **T**. Therefore, **T** is inconsistent.

By Church's Thesis, **T** is decidable iff the set of theorems of **T** is recursive. Let us define:

Def: **T** is *essentially undecidable* iff for every consistent theory **T*** containing **T**, **T*** is undecidable.

We then have:

(2.15)   **RR** is essentially undecidable.

Proof: Suppose **T** is a consistent theory containing **RR**. Then all recursive functions are representable in **T**, so Δ is weakly representable in **T**. If the set of theorems of **T** is recursive, then it is representable, and hence by (2.14), **T** is inconsistent. So **T** is not decidable.

This is a very profound result. It shows that *no* reasonably strong mathematical theory can be decidable, because any such theory will contain **RR**. Furthermore, it follows from (2.15) that the predicate calculus itself is not decidable. This is called ***Church's Theorem*** (not to be confused with Church's Thesis):

(2.16)   The set of valid formulas of the language of **RR** is not decidable.

Proof: **RR** has only finitely many axioms, so we can form their conjunction R. Then a formula P is a theorem of **RR** iff $\ulcorner R \supset P \urcorner$ is valid. Consequently, if validity were decidable, **RR** would be decidable.

The undecidability of the predicate calculus contrasts sharply with the decidability of the propositional calculus. In the case of the propositional calculus there is a simple decision procedure – truth tables. But Church's Theorem tells us that there is nothing analogous for the predicate calculus.

Various general conclusions can be drawn from this discussion of Gödel's theorem. It places major limits on the power of axiomatization. No reasonable set of axioms could be nonrecursive, and Gödel's theorem tells us that no even moderately strong first-order theory can be recursively axiomatized. In particular, no theory strong enough to provide a foundation for the rest of mathematics can be both consistent and recursively axiomatizable. Set theory is intended to provide just such a foundation. We were led to axiomatizations in set theory because our untutored intuitions turned out to be inconsistent. We now find that axiomatization cannot solve our problems in set theory. Any axiomatic set theory will be incomplete. Furthermore, by Gödel's second incompleteness theorem, if we could prove that an axiomatic set theory is consistent, and the set theory is strong enough to provide a foundation for mathematics, then the consistency proof could be carried out within the set theory itself, in which case it would actually follow that the set theory is inconsistent. So consistency proofs are worthless, and we are left with little more than untutored intuitions.

3. Higher-Order Logic

In first-order logic (the predicate calculus), quantifiers range over individuals. In higher-order logic, we introduce quantifiers over properties and relations as well, and we introduce "higher-order" properties of and relations between properties and relations. For instance, we can symbolize:

> John has some of his father's good characteristics

as

> $(\exists F)(Fj \ \& \ Ff \ \& \ G(F))$ (where f denotes John's father).

The most natural way to formulate higher-order logic is by introducing variables for properties and relations, allowing predicates and relations to occupy the argument places of other predicates and relations (as in $\ulcorner G(F) \urcorner$), and allowing quantifiers to incorporate variables for properties and relations. Higher-order logic might then be constructed on the basis of first-order logic and a single additional axiom scheme:

> For any n-formula $\psi(x_1,...,x_n)$ the following is an axiom:
> $(\exists R)(\forall x_1)...(\forall x_n)(Rx_1...x_n \equiv \psi(x_1,...,x_n))$.

Unfortunately, intuitive though this axiom is, it is inconsistent. This was first shown by Bertrand Russell. The argument goes as follows. Let us say that a property is *heterological* iff it does not exemplify itself:

Def: F is heterological iff $\sim F(F)$.

By the above axiom scheme, there is a property *Het* such that for any property F, F is heterological iff $Het(F)$. Now ask whether *Het* is heterological. We have:

> $Het(Het)$ iff *Het* is heterological
> iff $\sim Het(Het)$.

But this is a contradiction in the propositional calculus. The only principle employed in generating this contradiction is the above axiom scheme, so it is inconsistent. Notice that it is just a property-theoretic analogue of the axiom scheme of comprehension in set theory. That axiom scheme was shown to be inconsistent because of Russell's paradox, and the heterological paradox is a precise property-theoretic analogue of the latter.

This and similar paradoxes can be blocked by adopting a rigid hierarchy of properties and relations. *First-order properties and relations* are applicable exclusively to individuals. *Second-order properties and relations* are applicable exclusively to first-order properties and relations. In general, $(n+1)$-order properties and relations are applicable exclusively to n-order properties and relations. *Second-order logic* incorporates second-order properties and relations and quantification over first-order properties and relations. *ω-order* logic includes properties and relations of every order and quantification over them. This involves a rigid hierarchy of properties and relations. If a property applies to second-order properties, it cannot also apply to first-order properties or to individuals, and so on. It can be questioned whether such restrictions are reasonable, but this is the normal convention in higher-order logic.

The semantics for second-order logic is an extension of the semantics for first-order logic. Models are pairs $\langle D, \mu \rangle$ as before, but now μ must interpret second-order properties and relations as well as first-order properties and relations. First-order property variables are taken to range over all subsets of the domain. In other words, they range over possible extensions of first-order properties. Two-place relation variables range over subsets of the Cartesian product of the domain with itself, and so on. Second-order predicates that apply to first-order predicates are assigned extensions that are sets of subsets of the domain. Similarly for second-order predicates that apply to first-order relations. Second-order n-ary relation symbols are assigned extensions that are sets of n-tuples of extensions of first-order predicates or relations.

Second-order predicates and relation symbols are interpreted in terms of the extensions of the first-order properties and relations to which they apply. This requires them to be *extensional* in the sense that they cannot distinguish between two properties having the same extension or two relations having the same extension. For some purposes we might want to relax this assumption, but this is hard to do in standard second-order logic. It is perhaps best handled in modal logic.

Without going into the details, it should be obvious how truth in a model is to be defined. We then define validity, implication, and equivalence on analogy with the corresponding definitions in first-order logic.

It is natural to try to construct a system of derivations for second-order logic. A surprising consequence of Gödel's theorem is that this cannot be done. This results from our earlier discussion of Peano's axioms. In Chapter One, it was proven that any two relational structures satisfying Peano's axioms are isomorphic. That can be turned into a proof that any two models of Peano's (second-order) axioms **SS** are isomorphic. Isomorphic models make the same formulas true. Thus for any closed formula P, either P is true in every model of **SS** or $\sim P$ is true in every model of **SS**. Thus the set of formulas semantically implied by **SS** is complete. Gödel's theorem is easily reproduced for second-order logic in the following sense. Suppose there were a complete system of derivations for second-order logic. Then we could prove that if a consistent theory **T** contains **SS** and has a recursive set of axioms, "α is a proof of β" is representable in **T**, and hence **T** is incomplete. But **SS** is a consistent theory containing itself and having a recursive set of axioms, and **SS** is complete. Therefore, there can be no complete set of derivations for second-order logic. The same argument applies to ω-order logic.

In general, higher-order logic is significantly more powerful than first-order logic, but that power comes at considerable expense. First, the logic itself is not nearly so well behaved. In particular, there is no complete system of derivations for higher-order logic. Second, there are foundational difficulties for higher-order logic. The natural way of proceeding leads to inconsistencies, and the standard way of avoiding the inconsistencies—by imposing a rigid hierarchy of properties—seems excessively restrictive, and basically *ad hoc*. The foundational problems for higher-order logic are exactly parallel to the problems in the foundations of set theory, and might reasonably be regarded as variants of the same problems. However, the ingenuity that has gone into constructing interesting set theories has not been applied with equal enthusiasm to higher-order logic.

SOLUTIONS TO EXERCISES

Chapter One

(2.14) $A \subseteq B$ iff $A \cup B = B$.

Proof: Suppose $A \subseteq B$. To show that $A \cup B = B$, it suffices to show that $(\forall x)(x \in A \cup B \equiv x \in B)$. Suppose $x \in A \cup B$. Then $x \in$ IA or $x \in B$. As $A \subseteq B$, if $x \in A$ then $x \in B$, so in either case $x \in B$. Therefore, $x \in A \cup B \supset x \in B$. Conversely, suppose $x \in B$. Then $x \in A \vee x \in B$, so $x \in A \cup B$. Thus $x \in A \cup B \equiv x \in B$.

   Conversely, suppose $A \cup B = B$. $A \subseteq A \cup B$, so as $A \cup B = B$, $A \subseteq B$.

(2.16) $A \subseteq C \ \& \ B \subseteq C$ iff $A \cup B \subseteq C$.

Proof: Suppose $A \subseteq C \ \& \ B \subseteq C$. Suppose $x \in A \cup B$. Then $x \in A$ or $x \in B$, and in either case $x \in C$. Thus $A \cup B \subseteq C$. Conversely, suppose $A \cup B \subseteq C$. $A \subseteq A \cup B$, so by transitivity (theorem (2.3)), $A \subseteq C$. Similarly, $B \subseteq C$.

(2.20) $A - (B \cap C) = (A-B) \cup (A-C)$.

Proof: $x \in A - (B \cap C)$ iff $x \in A \ \& \ x \notin (B \cap C)$
                   iff $x \in A \ \& \ (x \notin B \vee x \notin C)$
                   iff $(x \in A \ \& \ x \notin B) \vee (x \in A \ \& \ x \notin C)$
                   iff $x \in (A-B) \vee x \in (A-C)$
                   iff $x \in (A-B) \cup (A-C)$.

(2.26) $\mathbf{P}(A \cap B) = \mathbf{P}(A) \cap \mathbf{P}(B)$.

Proof: $X \in \mathbf{P}(A \cap B)$ iff $X \subseteq (A \cap B)$
                   iff $X \subseteq A \ \& \ X \subseteq B$ (by (2.15))
                   iff $X \in \mathbf{P}(A) \ \& \ X \in \mathbf{P}(B)$
                   iff $X \in \mathbf{P}(A) \cap \mathbf{P}(B)$.

Exercise: It is not always true that $P(A \cup B) = P(A \cup B)$. What are simple necessary and sufficient conditions for this identity to hold?

Answer: $P(A \cup B) = P(A \cup B)$ iff $(A \subseteq B) \vee (B \subseteq A)$.
Proof: Suppose $A \subseteq B$. Then $A \cup B = B$, and by (2.25), $P(A) \subseteq P(B)$, so $P(A) \cup P(B) = P(B) = P(A \cup B)$. Similarly, if $B \subseteq A$ then $P(A) \cup P(B) = P(A \cup B)$. Conversely, suppose $A \not\subseteq B$ & $B \not\subseteq A$. Then there is some x such that $x \in A$ & $x \notin B$, and there is some y such that $y \in B$ & $y \notin A$. Then $\{x,y\} \not\subseteq A$ and $\{x,y\} \not\subseteq B$, so $\{x,y\} \notin P(A) \cup P(B)$. But $\{x,y\} \subseteq A \cup B$, so $\{x,y\} \in P(A \cup B)$. Thus $P(A) \cup P(B) \neq P(A \cup B)$.

(2.29) $\bigcup \{A\} = A$.

Proof: $x \in \bigcup \{A\}$ iff x is a member of some member of $\{A\}$. But the only member of $\{A\}$ is A, so $x \in \bigcup \{A\}$ iff $x \in A$, i.e., $\bigcup \{A\} = A$.

(2.31)   If $H \subseteq K$ then $\bigcup H \subseteq \bigcup K$.

Proof: Suppose $H \subseteq K$. Suppose $x \in \bigcup H$. Then for some Y in H, $x \in Y$. But if $Y \in H$ then $Y \in K$, so $x \in \bigcup K$.

(2.33) $\bigcap \{A\} = A$.

Proof: $x \in \bigcap \{A\}$ iff x is a member of every member of $\{A\}$. But the only member of $\{A\}$ is A, so $x \in \bigcap \{A\}$ iff $x \in A$, i.e., $\bigcap \{A\} = A$.

(2.34)   If $H \subseteq K$ then $\bigcap K \subseteq \bigcap H$.

Proof: Suppose $H \subseteq K$. Suppose $x \in \bigcap K$. Then x is in every member of K. But every member of H is a member of K, so x is in every member of H. That is, $x \in \bigcap H$.

(2.35)   If $A \in K$ then $\bigcap K \subseteq A$.

Proof: Suppose $A \in K$. Suppose $x \in \bigcap K$. Then x is in every member of K. But one such member is A, so $x \in K$.

(2.36)   If $(\forall X)(X \in K \supset A \subseteq X)$ then $A \subseteq \bigcap K$.

Proof: Suppose $(\forall X)(X \in K \supset A \subseteq X)$. Suppose $x \in A$. Then if $X \in K$, as $A \subseteq X$, $x \in X$. So x is a member of every member of K, i.e., $x \in \bigcap K$. Thus $A \subseteq \bigcap K$.

(3.4)   If $A \neq \emptyset$ & $B \neq \emptyset$ then $A \times B = C \times D$ iff $A = C$ & $B = D$.

Proof: Suppose $A \neq \emptyset$ & $B \neq \emptyset$. Trivially, if $A = C$ and $B = D$ then $A \times B = C \times D$. Conversely, suppose $A \times B = C \times D$. Then for any pair $\langle x,y \rangle$, $\langle x,y \rangle \in A \times B \equiv \langle x,y \rangle \in C \times D$. Suppose $x \in A$. Choose any y in B. Then $\langle x,y \rangle \in A \times B$, so $\langle x,y \rangle \in C \times D$. But then $x \in C$. Therefore, $A \subseteq C$. Similarly, $C \subseteq A$, $B \subseteq D$, and $D \subseteq C$.

(3.5) $A \times (B \cup C) = (A \times B) \cup (A \times C)$.

Proof: $\langle x,y \rangle \in A \times (B \cup C)$ iff $x \in A$ & $(y \in B \vee y \in C)$
iff $(x \in A$ & $y \in B) \vee (x \in A$ & $y \in C)$
iff $\langle x,y \rangle \in A \times B \vee \langle x,y \rangle \in A \times C$
iff $\langle x,y \rangle (A \times B) \cup (A \times C)$.

(3.7) $R^*(A \cup B) = R^*(A) \cup R^*(B)$.

Proof: Suppose $y \in R^*(A \cup B)$. Then for some x in $(A \cup B)$, xRy. $x \in A$ or $x \in B$, so $y \in R^*(A)$ or $y \in R^*(B)$, and hence $y \in R^*(A) \cup R^*(B)$. Conversely, suppose $y \in R^*(A) \cup R^*(B)$. Then either there is an x in A such that xRy or there is an x in B such that xRy. In either case, $x \in A \cup B$, so $y \in R^*(A \cup B)$.

(3.8)   If $A \subseteq B$ then $R^*(A) \subseteq R^*(B)$.

Proof: Suppose $A \subseteq B$. Suppose $y \in R^*(A)$. Then for some x in A, xRy. As $A \subseteq B$, $y \in B$, so $y \in R^*(B)$.

(3.10) $(A \times B)^{-1} = (B \times A)$.

Proof: $\langle x,y \rangle \in (A \times B)^{-1}$ iff $\langle y,x \rangle \in (A \times B)$
iff $y \in B$ & $x \in A$
iff $x \in A$ & $y \in B$
iff $\langle x,y \rangle \in (A \times B)$.

(3.13)   If R is asymmetric then R is irreflexive.

Proof: Suppose R is asymmetric. Then for any x and y, $xRy \supset {\sim}yRx$. So in particular, $xRx \supset {\sim}xRx$. This is equivalent, by the propositional calculus, to ${\sim}xRx$.

(3.16)   If R is an equivalence relation and $x,y \in F(R)$ and $R^*\{x\}$ $\neq R^*\{y\}$ then $R^*\{x\} \cap R^*\{y\} = \emptyset$.

Proof: Suppose R is an equivalence relation and $x,y \in F(R)$ and $R^*\{x\}$ $\neq R^*\{y\}$. Suppose $z \in R^*\{x\} \cap R^*\{y\}$. Then xRz & yRz. By symmetry, zRy, so by transitivity and the fact that xRz, it follows that xRz. Then by (3.15), $R^*\{x\} = R^*\{y\}$, which is contrary to the initial supposition. Thus there can be no z in $R^*\{x\} \cap R^*\{y\}$, i.e., $R^*\{x\} \cap R^*\{y\} = \emptyset$.

(3.17)   If R is a strict simple ordering then $R \cup \{\langle x,x \rangle \mid x \in F(R)\}$ is a simple ordering.

Proof: Suppose R is a strict simple ordering. By definition, R is transitive, asymmetric, and connected. It must be shown that $R \cup \{\langle x,x \rangle \mid x \in F(R)\}$ is transitive, reflexive, antisymmetric, and strongly connected.

   (a)   Suppose $\langle x,y \rangle \in R \cup \{\langle x,x \rangle \mid x \in F(R)\}$ and $\langle y,z \rangle \in R \cup \{\langle x,x \rangle \mid$ $x \in F(R)\}$. Then either (*i*) $\langle x,y \rangle \in R$ or (*ii*) $x = y$, and either (*iii*) $\langle y,z \rangle \in R$ or (*iv*) $y = z$. If (*i*) and (*iii*) then $\langle x,z \rangle \in R$ by the transitivity of R, so $\langle x,z \rangle \in R \cup \{\langle x,x \rangle \mid x \in F(R)\}$. If (*i*) and (*iv*) then $\langle x,y \rangle \in R$ and y $= z$, so $\langle x,z \rangle \in R$, and hence $\langle x,z \rangle \in R \cup \{\langle x,x \rangle \mid x \in F(R)\}$. The proof is analogous if (*ii*) and (*iii*). If (*ii*) and (*iv*) then $x = y = z = w$, so $x = z$ and hence $\langle x,z \rangle \in R \cup \{\langle x,x \rangle \mid x \in F(R)\}$. Thus in each case, $\langle x,z \rangle \in R \cup \{\langle x,x \rangle \mid x \in F(R)\}$, so $R \cup \{\langle x,x \rangle \mid x \in F(R)\}$ is transitive.

   (b) $F(R \cup \{\langle x,x \rangle \mid x \in F(R)\}) = F(R)$, so if $x \in F(R \cup \{\langle x,x \rangle \mid$ $x \in F(R)\})$ then $\langle x,x \rangle \in R \cup \{\langle x,x \rangle \mid x \in F(R)\}$, and hence $R \cup \{\langle x,x \rangle \mid$ $x \in F(R)\}$ is reflexive.

   (c)   Suppose $x \neq y$ and $\langle x,y \rangle \in R \cup \{\langle x,x \rangle \mid x \in F(R)\}$. Then $\langle x,y \rangle \in R$. R is asymmetric, so $\langle y,x \rangle \notin R$. Thus $\langle y,x \rangle \notin R \cup \{\langle x,x \rangle \mid x \in F(R)\}$, and hence $R \cup \{\langle x,x \rangle \mid x \in F(R)\}$ is antisymmetric.

   (d)   Suppose $\langle x,y \rangle \in F(R \cup \{\langle x,x \rangle \mid x \in F(R)\})$. Then $\langle x,y \rangle \in F(R)$. R is connected, so either $x = y$ or $\langle x,y \rangle \in R$ or $\langle y,x \rangle \in R$. Therefore, either $\langle x,y \rangle \in R \cup \{\langle x,x \rangle \mid x \in F(R)\}$ or $\langle y,x \rangle \in R \cup \{\langle x,x \rangle \mid x \in F(R)\}$. Hence, $R \cup \{\langle x,x \rangle \mid x \in F(R)\}$ is strongly connected.

(3.18) If R is a simple ordering then $R\text{-}\{\langle x,x \rangle \mid x \in \mathbf{F}(R)\}$ is a strict simple ordering.

Proof: Suppose R is a simple ordering. Then R is transitive, reflexive, antisymmetric, and strongly connected. It must be shown that $R\text{-}\{\langle x,x \rangle \mid x \in \mathbf{F}(R)\}$ is transitive, asymmetric, and connected.

(a) Suppose $\langle x,y \rangle \in R\text{-}\{\langle x,x \rangle \mid x \in \mathbf{F}(R)\}$ and $\langle y,z \rangle \in R\text{-}\{\langle x,x \rangle \mid x \in \mathbf{F}(R)\}$. Then $\langle x,y \rangle \in R$ and $\langle y,z \rangle \in R$ and $x \neq y$ and $y \neq z$. By the transitivity of R, $\langle x,z \rangle \in R$. If $x = z$ then zRy and yRz, which is impossible as R is antisymmetric. So $x \neq z$. Hence $\langle x,z \rangle \in R\text{-}\{\langle x,x \rangle \mid x \in \mathbf{F}(R)\}$. Therefore, $R\text{-}\{\langle x,x \rangle \mid x \in \mathbf{F}(R)\}$ is transitive.

(b) Suppose $\langle x,y \rangle \in R\text{-}\{\langle x,x \rangle \mid x \in \mathbf{F}(R)\}$. Then $\langle x,y \rangle \in R$ and $x \neq y$. R is antisymmetric, so $\langle y,x \rangle \notin R$. Thus $\langle y,x \rangle \notin R\text{-}\{\langle x,x \rangle \mid x \in \mathbf{F}(R)\}$. Therefore, $R\text{-}\{\langle x,x \rangle \mid x \in \mathbf{F}(R)\}$ is asymmetric.

(c) Suppose $\langle x,y \rangle \in \mathbf{F}(R\text{-}\{\langle x,x \rangle \mid x \in \mathbf{F}(R)\})$ and $x \neq y$. $\mathbf{F}(R\text{-}\{\langle x,x \rangle \mid x \in \mathbf{F}(R)\}) = \mathbf{F}(R)$, so $\langle x,y \rangle \in \mathbf{F}(R)$. R is strongly connected, so $\langle x,y \rangle \in R$ or $\langle y,x \rangle \in R$. Then $\langle x,y \rangle \in R\text{-}\{\langle x,x \rangle \mid x \in \mathbf{F}(R)\}$ or $\langle y,x \rangle \in R\text{-}\{\langle x,x \rangle \mid x \in \mathbf{F}(R)\}$, so $R\text{-}\{\langle x,x \rangle \mid x \in \mathbf{F}(R)\}$ is connected.

(4.4) If $\langle A,R \rangle$ and $\langle B,S \rangle$ are relational structures and $\langle A,R \rangle \approx_f \langle B,S \rangle$, then R is a simple ordering of A iff S is a simple ordering of B.

Proof: Suppose $\langle A,R \rangle \approx_f \langle B,S \rangle$. We must show that if R is reflexive, antisymmetric, and connected, then S is too (we have already dealt with transitivity). We take these one at a time:

(a) Suppose R is reflexive. Suppose $x \in B$. xSx iff $f^{-1}(x)Rf^{-1}(x)$, but the latter holds by reflexivity.

(b) Suppose R is antisymmetric. Suppose $x,y \in B$, $x \neq y$, and xSy. Then $f^{-1}(x)Rf^{-1}(x)$. f is 1-1, so $f^{-1}(x) \neq f^{-1}(y)$, and thus as R is antisymmetric, $\sim[f^{-1}(y)Rf^{-1}(x)]$. Hence $\sim ySx$.

(c) Suppose R is connected. Suppose $x,y \in B$ and $x \neq y$. Then $f^{-1}(x) \neq f^{-1}(y)$, so as R is connected, $f^{-1}(x)Rf^{-1}(y)$ or $f^{-1}(y)Rf^{-1}(x)$. Then xSy or ySx.

(5.7) If $x \in \mathbf{C}_{\{R\}}(A_0)$ then either $x \in A_0$ or $x \in R^*A_0$ or for some y in $x \in \mathbf{C}_{\{R\}}(R^*A_0)$, yRx.

Proof by set-theoretic induction:
Basis step: Suppose $x \in A_0$. Then trivially $x \in A_0$ or $x \in R^*A_0$ or for some y in $\mathbf{C}_{\{R\}}(R^*A_0)$, yRx.

Induction step: Suppose $x \in A_0$ or $x \in R^*A_0$ or for some z in $x \in C_{\{R\}}(R^*A_0)$, zRx, and show that if xRy then either $x \in A_0$ or $x \in R^*A_0$ or for some z in $C_{\{R\}}(R^*A_0)$, zRy. We prove this by cases:

(a) Suppose $x \in A_0$ and xRy. Then $y \in R^*A_0$.

(b) Suppose $x \in R^*A_0$ and xRy. Then $x \in C_{\{R\}}(R^*A_0)$, so for some z (namely, x itself) in $C_{\{R\}}(R^*A_0)$, zRy.

(c) Suppose that for some z in $C_{\{R\}}(R^*A_0)$, zRx, and xRy. $C_{\{R\}}(R^*A_0)$ is closed under R so $x \in C_{\{R\}}(R^*A_0)$. Hence for some z (namely, x itself) in $C_{\{R\}}(R^*A_0)$, zRy.

(6.10)   If $n \in \omega$ & $n \neq 0$ then $0 < n$.

Proof by mathematical induction:

Basis step: $0 = 0$, so it is vacuously true that if $0 \neq 0$ then $0 < 0$.

Induction step: Suppose $[(n \in \omega$ & $n \neq 0) \supset 0 < n]$. Suppose $\sim(0 < S(n))$. Then by (6.6), $S(n) \neq S(0)$ and $\sim(\exists y)(0 < y$ & $S(n) = S(y))$. If $n = 0$ then $S(n) = S(0)$, so $n \neq 0$. Then by the induction hypothesis, $0 < n$. But then there is a y (namely, n) such that $0 < y$ & $S(n) = S(y)$. So we have a contradiction, and hence it cannot have been the case that $\sim(0 < S(n))$.

(6.11)   If $n \in \omega$ then $0 < S(n)$.

Proof: Suppose $n \in \omega$. By (6.10), either $n = 0$ or $0 < n$. If $n = 0$ then $S(n) = S(0)$, so as $0 < S(0)$, $0 < S(n)$. If instead $0 < n$, then as $n < S(n)$, $0 < S(n)$.

(6.24)   If $n, m \in \omega$ then $n < m$ iff $n \subset m$.

Proof by mathematical induction that for each n, $(\forall m)(m < n \supset m \subset n)$:

Basis step: Nothing can be a member of (i.e., less than) $\varnothing$, so it is vacuously true that $(\forall m)(m < 0 \supset m \subset 0)$.

Induction step: Suppose $(\forall m)(m < n \supset m \subset n)$. Suppose $m < S(n)$, i.e., $m \in n \cup \{n\}$. Then $m \in n$ or $m = n$. Suppose $m \in n$, i.e., $m < n$. Then by the induction hypothesis, $m \subset n$. But $n \subseteq S(n)$, so $m \subset S(n)$. Suppose instead that $m = n$. $n \subseteq n \cup \{n\} = S(n)$. If $n = n \cup \{n\}$ then $n \in n$, but this is precluded by (6.21). So $n \subsetneq S(n)$, and as $m = n$, $m \subsetneq S(n)$.

The converse was proven in the text.

Chapter Two

(1.5)   A closed formula is valid iff its negation is unsatisfiable.

Proof: A closed formula P is valid iff P is true in every model, iff $\sim P$ is false in every model, iff $\sim P$ is unsatisfiable.

(1.7) $\models P$ iff $\emptyset \models P$.

Proof: $\emptyset \models P$ iff P is true in every model of $\emptyset$. Every model is a model of $\emptyset$, because every model makes every member of $\emptyset$ true. Thus $\emptyset \models P$ iff P is true in every model, i.e., iff $\models P$.

(1.10)   If P is equivalent to Q then $\sim P$ is equivalent to $\sim Q$.

Proof: Suppose P is equivalent to Q. Then they have the same extensions, and they contain free occurrences of the same variables. $\sim P$ and $\sim Q$ also contain free occurrences of those same variables. For any model $\langle D, \mu \rangle$, the extension of $\sim P$ in $\langle D, \mu \rangle$ is the set of all n-tuples of members of D that are not in the extension of P, and similarly for $\sim Q$. Thus $\sim P$ has the same extension in $\langle D, \mu \rangle$ is $\sim Q$. This is true for every model $\langle D, \mu \rangle$, so $\sim P$ is equivalent to Q.

(1.11)   If P is equivalent to Q then $\ulcorner(P \ \& \ R)\urcorner$ is equivalent to $\ulcorner(Q \ \& \ R)\urcorner$ and $\ulcorner(R \ \& \ Q)\urcorner$ is equivalent to $\ulcorner(R \ \& \ P)\urcorner$.

Proof: Suppose P is equivalent to Q. Then they contain free occurrences of the same variables. It follows that $\ulcorner(P \ \& \ R)\urcorner$ and $\ulcorner(Q \ \& \ R)\urcorner$ also contain free occurrences of the same variables $x_1,...,x_n$. Choose constants $a_1,...,a_n$ not occurring in P, Q, or R. By (1.8), $\ulcorner(P \ \& \ R)\urcorner$ is equivalent to $\ulcorner(Q \ \& \ R)\urcorner$ iff $Sb(a_1,...,a_n/x_1,...,x_n)\ulcorner(P \ \& \ R)\urcorner$ is equivalent to $Sb(a_1,...,a_n/x_1,...,x_n)\ulcorner(Q \ \& \ R)\urcorner$. For any model $\langle D, \mu \rangle$, $Sb(a_1,...,a_n/x_1,...,x_n)\ulcorner(P \ \& \ R)\urcorner$ is true in $\langle D, \mu \rangle$ iff $Sb(a_1,...,a_n/x_1,...,x_n)P$ and $Sb(a_1,...,a_n/x_1,...,x_n)R$ are both true. By (1.18), $Sb(a_1,...,a_n/x_1,...,x_n)P$ and $Sb(a_1,...,a_n/x_1,...,x_n)Q$ are equivalent, so $Sb(a_1,...,a_n/x_1,...,x_n)P$ is true in $\langle D, \mu \rangle$ iff $Sb(a_1,...,a_n/x_1,...,x_n)Q$ is true in $\langle D, \mu \rangle$. Thus $Sb(a_1,...,a_n/x_1,...,x_n)\ulcorner(P \ \& \ R)\urcorner$ is true in $\langle D, \mu \rangle$ iff $Sb(a_1,...,a_n/x_1,...,x_n)Q$ and $Sb(a_1,...,a_n/x_1,...,x_n)R$ are both true, which holds iff $Sb(a_1,...,a_n/x_1,...,x_n)\ulcorner(Q \ \& \ R)\urcorner$ is true in

$\langle D,\mu \rangle$. Therefore, $Sb(a_1,...,a_n/x_1,...,x_n)\ulcorner(P \; \& \; R)\urcorner$ is equivalent to $Sb(a_1,...,a_n/x_1,...,x_n)\ulcorner(Q \; \& \; R)\urcorner$, and hence $\ulcorner(P \; \& \; R)\urcorner$ is equivalent to $\ulcorner(Q \; \& \; R)\urcorner$.

(1.12) If P is equivalent to Q then $\ulcorner(\exists x)P\urcorner$ is equivalent to $\ulcorner(\exists x)Q\urcorner$.

Proof: Suppose P is equivalent to Q. Then they have the same extensions, and they contain free occurrences of the same variables x and $x_1,...,x_n$. $\ulcorner(\exists x)P\urcorner$ and $\ulcorner(\exists x)Q\urcorner$ then contain free occurrences of the same variables $x_1,...,x_n$. For any model $\langle D,\mu \rangle$, the extension of $\ulcorner(\exists x)P\urcorner$ in $\langle D,\mu \rangle$ is the set of all n-tuples $\langle \alpha_1,...,\alpha_n \rangle$ such that there is an α in D for which $\langle \alpha,\alpha_1,...,\alpha_n \rangle$ satisfies P, and similarly for $\ulcorner(\exists x)Q\urcorner$. Thus $\ulcorner(\exists x)P\urcorner$ and $\ulcorner(\exists x)Q\urcorner$ have the same extensions in any model $\langle D,\mu \rangle$, and so they are equivalent.

(1.15) If a system of derivations is strongly sound then it is sound, and if it is strongly complete then it is complete.

Proof: The first half of the theorem was proven in the text. For the second half, suppose a system of derivations is strongly complete. Suppose $\models P$. Then by (1.7), $\emptyset \models P$. It follows by strong completeness that $\emptyset \vdash P$, and hence by definition, $\vdash P$.

(1.16) PC-derivations are strongly sound iff every satisfiable set of closed formulas is consistent, and PC-derivations are strongly complete iff every consistent set of closed formulas is satisfiable.

Proof: Suppose PC-derivations are strongly sound. Suppose Γ is inconsistent. Then for some Q, $\Gamma \vdash (Q \; \& \; {\sim}Q)$. As PC-derivations are strongly sound, $\Gamma \models (Q \; \& \; {\sim}Q)$. Thus every model of Γ is a model of $(Q \; \& \; {\sim}Q)$. But $(Q \; \& \; {\sim}Q)$ has no models, so Γ has no models, i.e., Γ is unsatisfiable.

Conversely, suppose every satisfiable set of closed formulas is consistent. If it is not the case that $\Gamma \models P$, then $\Gamma \cup \{{\sim}P\}$ is satisfiable, and hence by supposition, $\Gamma \cup \{{\sim}P\}$ is consistent. Therefore, it is not the case that $\Gamma \vdash P$. Thus if $\Gamma \vdash P$ then $\Gamma \models P$, i.e., PC-derivations are strongly sound.

Similarly, suppose PC-derivations are strongly complete.

Suppose Γ is unsatisfiable. Then $\Gamma \models (P \ \& \sim P)$, so $\Gamma \vdash (P \ \& \sim P)$, and hence Γ is inconsistent.

Conversely, suppose every consistent set of closed formulas is satisfiable. If it is not the case that $\Gamma \vdash P$, then $\Gamma \cup \{\sim P\}$ is consistent, and hence by supposition, $\Gamma \cup \{\sim P\}$ is satisfiable. Therefore, it is not the case that $\Gamma \models P$. Thus if $\Gamma \models P$ then $\Gamma \vdash P$, i.e., PC-derivations are strongly complete.

(1.23)   If Γ is maximal consistent and P and Q are closed formulas then $\ulcorner(P \ \& \ Q)\urcorner \in \Gamma$ iff $P \in \Gamma$ and $Q \in \Gamma$.

Proof: Suppose Γ is maximal consistent and P and Q are closed formulas. If $\ulcorner(P \ \& \ Q)\urcorner \in \Gamma$, then by (1.21), $P \in \Gamma$ and $Q \in \Gamma$. Conversely, suppose $P \in \Gamma$ and $Q \in \Gamma$. If $\ulcorner(P \ \& \ Q)\urcorner \notin \Gamma$ then $\ulcorner\sim(P \ \& \ Q)\urcorner \in \Gamma$, but then Γ would be inconsistent. So $\ulcorner(P \ \& \ Q)\urcorner \in \Gamma$.

(2.1)   If **T** is an interpreted first-order theory then:
    (a)   if **T** is sound, then **T** is complete iff **T** is semantically complete;
    (b)   if **T** is unsound, then if **T** is consistent, it is semantically incomplete;
    (c)   if **T** is semantically complete, then **T** is sound iff **T** is consistent.

Proof: (a) was proven in the text.

(b) Suppose **T** is unsound and consistent. As **T** is unsound, there is some closed formula P false in the intended model that is a theorem of **T**. If **T** were semantically complete, $\sim P$ would have to be a theorem of **T** as well, in which case **T** would be inconsistent.

(c) Suppose **T** is semantically complete. If **T** is inconsistent, then for some closed formula P, both P and $\sim P$ are theorems of **T**, in which case **T** is unsound. Conversely, suppose **T** is unsound. Then for some closed formula P, P is false in the intended model but P is a theorem of **T**. In that case, $\sim P$ is true in the intended model, so by semantical completeness, $\sim P$ is a theorem of **T**, and hence **T** is inconsistent.

(2.5)   If Δ is weakly representable in **T**, then given any 1-formula $\psi(x)$ there is a closed formula θ such that $\ulcorner\theta \equiv \psi(\eta(\theta))\urcorner$ is a theorem of **T**.

Proof: Suppose $\delta(x)$ weakly represents Δ.   Let $\theta =$ $\psi(\delta(\eta(\psi(\delta(x)))))$. $\Delta(\psi(\delta(x))) = \psi(\delta(\eta(\psi(\delta(x)))))$, so as δ weakly represents Δ, $\ulcorner \delta(\eta(\psi(\delta(x)))) = \eta(\psi(\delta(\eta(\psi(\delta(x))))))\urcorner$ is a theorem of T. That is, $\ulcorner \delta(\eta(\psi(\delta(x)))) = \eta(\theta)\urcorner$ is a theorem of T. Trivially, $\ulcorner \psi(\delta(\eta(\psi(\delta(x))))) \equiv \psi(\delta(\eta(\psi(\delta(x)))))\urcorner$ is a theorem of T, so by the substitutivity of identity, substituting $\eta(\theta)$ for $\ulcorner \delta(\eta(\psi(\delta(x))))\urcorner$ in this biconditional, we obtain that $\ulcorner \psi(\delta(\eta(\psi(\delta(x))))) \equiv \psi(\eta(\theta))\urcorner$ is a theorem of T. But this is just $\ulcorner \theta \equiv \psi(\eta(\theta))\urcorner$.

SYMBOLS

Technical symbols are listed in order of their introduction.

$(\forall x)$ universal quantifier 1
$(\exists x)$ existential quantifier 1
$\&$ conjunction 1
$\vee$ disjunction 1
$\supset$ conditional 1
$\equiv$ biconditional 1
$\sim$ negation 1
$=$ identity 1
$\in$ membership 2
iff if and only if 2
$\emptyset$ empty set 5
$\subseteq$ subset 6
$\subset$ proper subset 8
$\cup$ union 8
$\cap$ intersection 9
$A-B$ relative complement 11
$\mathbf{P}(A)$ power set 12
$\bigcup K$ generalized union 13
$\bigcap K$ generalized intersection 13
$\langle x,y \rangle$ ordered pair 15
$A \times B$ Cartesian product 17
$\mathbf{D}(R)$ domain 21
$\mathbf{R}(R)$ range 21
$\mathbf{F}(R)$ field 22
R^*A R-image 22
R^{-1} converse 22
R/S relative product 23
$f:A \longrightarrow B$ mapping into 33

INDEX

absolute provability 96
adjunctivity 75
algorithm 102
ancestral 40,43
antisymmetry 24
arithmetic 59
assignment 67
asymmetry 23
atomic formula 64
axiom 73
axiom of comprehension 3
axiom of extensionality 2
axiom scheme of induction 95
axiomatic theories 87
axiomatization of a theory 88

basis step 42,46
bound occurrence of a variable 65

Cartesian product 17
categorical set of axioms 54
characteristic function 102
Church's theorem 105
Church's thesis 102
class inclusion 6
class membership 2
closed formula 65
compactness theorem 84
complement 11

complete system of derivations 77
complete theory 89
composition of functions 33
connectedness 24
consistent set of formulas 75
consistent theory 88
contradiction 75
converse of a relation 22
corner quotes 63
crisis in set theory 99

De Morgan's laws 11
decidable set 102
decidable theory 105
definite description 84
definition by abstraction 3
definitions 37
denotation of a constant 67
denumerable set 80
derivable formula 75
derivations 72ff
diagonal function 92
disjoint sets 9
domain 21,32
double negation 75

elements 2
elimination rule 75
empty set 5
equivalence 69,70

1-9/00